IMAGES
of America

RICHMOND'S FIRST AFRICAN BAPTIST CHURCH

THE PASTOR IN HIS STUDY. Dr. Rodney D. Waller follows in a long and honorable tradition as the senior pastor of the venerable First African Baptist Church of Richmond, which can trace its origins to 1780. (Courtesy of the First African Baptist Church.)

ON THE COVER: FIRST AFRICAN BAPTIST CHURCH, 1865. When the First Baptist Church congregation sold their meetinghouse on Cary and Second Streets, the church was moved to College and Broad Streets, where the original structure pictured was built in 1802. It was located on land purchased from Dr. Philip Turpin and twice enlarged until it appeared as pictured in this image captured shortly after Richmond's liberation by Union troops on April 3, 1865. As the White members of First Baptist moved two blocks west to Twelfth and Broad Streets, the Black congregants were allocated the old building and constituted in 1841 as First African Baptist Church. The building was demolished in 1876 amidst some controversy. (Courtesy of the Library of Congress.)

IMAGES
of America

RICHMOND'S FIRST AFRICAN BAPTIST CHURCH

Dr. Raymond Pierre Hylton,
Dr. Rodney D. Waller,
and Dr. Kimberly A. Matthews

ARCADIA
PUBLISHING

Published by Arcadia Publishing
Charleston, South Carolina

Printed in the United States of America

Library of Congress Control Number: 2022943655

For all general information, please contact Arcadia Publishing:
Telephone 843-853-2070
Fax 843-853-0044
E-mail sales@arcadiapublishing.com
For customer service and orders:
Toll-Free 1-888-313-2665

Visit us on the Internet at www.arcadiapublishing.com

I dedicate this book to my parents, Albert and Lindell Matthews

—KAM

*To Mary Claire Hylton, Nicole DeVizcaya Hylton,
Madeleine Henriet Marchal, Thomas Preston Hylton,
Alice Henrietta Whitrow, and Eric Hugh Whitrow*

—RPH

I dedicate this book to my mom, Vera E. Jenkins Waller, with all my love.

—RDW

CONTENTS

Acknowledgments   6

Introduction   7

1.   In the Shadow of Slavery: 1780–1865   9

2.   In the Era of James Henry Holmes: 1865–1900   31

3.   In the Early 20th Century: 1900–1950   53

4.   In the Later 20th Century: 1950–2000   85

5.   In the 21st Century: 2000–2021   103

Bibliography   127

ACKNOWLEDGMENTS

The images are courtesy of First African Baptist Church (FABC); the Library of Congress (LOC);the Virginia Union University Archives (VUU); the University of Virginia (UVA); Virginia Commonwealth University (VCU); the Valentine History Center (VHC); the *Richmond Times-Dispatch* (RTD); the *Richmond Free Press* (RFP); the Virginia Department of Historical Resources (VDHR); the Henrico County Department of Historical Resources (HDHR); the National Parks Service (NPS); the Boatwright Library, University of Richmond; the Boston Public Library; the New York Public Library; the Library of Virginia (LOV); and indicated individuals.

INTRODUCTION

In 1780, the city of Richmond, Virginia, had been in existence for 43 years. In April that year, it had been "upscaled" to becoming the state's new capital, replacing Williamsburg. The Revolutionary War was raging, and Richmond, located farther inland, was considered less vulnerable to attacks by the British (though they captured it anyway on January 5, 1781). Barely noticed at the time, members of the Baptist faith who had originally worshipped at Boar Swamp, in what is now Henrico County, were organized by Pastor Joshua Morris and met at the home of John Franklin at the corner of Carrington and Pink Streets. This was the unobtrusive genesis for the First Baptist Church of Richmond. It had to be low-profiled because Baptist worshippers were still liable to penalties under Virginia law. Baptists had been imprisoned as late as 1778, and the Church of England remained the legally established church until 1786, when the Virginia Act for Religious Freedom guaranteed toleration for Baptists and other dissenters.

Even less noticed was the birth, some 25 miles east of Richmond in Charles City County, of a slave child named Lott Carey. Later, the fates of both Carey and First Baptist Church would intertwine. Overlooked was the presence of Black congregants, both slave and free. While the pastors and church leaders were entirely White, the disparity in numbers widened until by 1800 the ratio of Black over White membership was three to one. As a new century began, certain African American church members started to attract notice. Lott Carey purchased his freedom and emerged as a pioneering missionary to West Africa. Gilbert Hunt became one of Richmond's most celebrated heroes, and young Henry Brown planned a daring bid for freedom that would stun the world and accelerate the momentum of the abolitionist movement.

Neither Virginia, Richmond, nor the First Baptist Church could isolate itself from the growing North-South sectional rift and its principal underlying cause, the institution of slavery. The crisis deepened and finally erupted into conflict. The Civil War (or "Jubilee War"—a term that some historians employ to indicate slavery/emancipation as the conflict's primary focus and result) would cost between 600,000 and 700,000 lives.

In 1780, the slavery-based economy was less lucrative than it had been, particularly in the upper-southern states such as Virginia. But the invention of the cotton gin in 1793 made plantation slavery profitable again. The opening of vast traces of acreage to cotton cultivation from South Carolina to Texas sparked an economic boom and demand for more slave labor. Virginia became the leading supplier of slaves for the internal slave trade to the Deep South. Richmond became a major center for this trade, with large slave auctioning and prison facilities in Shockoe Valley forming an integral part of the city's economy. Groups of slaves shackled together, forced to walk to places like Alabama and Mississippi, became a common sight on roads and highways—the infamous "slave coffles."

The slave insurrection in Haiti; Gabriel Prosser's conspiracy in Richmond (1800); Charles Deslondes's German Coast uprising near New Orleans, Louisiana (1811); Denmark Vesey's conspiracy in Charleston, South Carolina (1822); and especially Nat Turner's rebellion in Southampton

County, Virginia (1831), forced the issue to the center of the political stage. Debating the issue of gradual emancipation as opposed to even more restrictive measures of control over both slave and freed Blacks, the General Assembly voted for the second, repressive option.

At First Baptist Church, overcrowded conditions within the church building on College and Broad Streets impelled the congregation to split and form two churches, segregated by race. The White congregants moved to a new building at Twelfth and Broad Streets, while the African American worshipers stayed in the old premises. On July 1, 1841, First African Baptist Church was inaugurated.

From 1841 to 1865, First African operated under a white pastor, Dr. Robert Ryland (African Americans being legally excluded from the ministry), and briefly (1865–1866) under another white minister, abolitionist George S. Stockwell. But the liberation of Richmond and the abolition of slavery would bring about change. The racially based state regulations ended, and in 1866, the congregation elected its first Black pastor, James Henry Holmes. Holmes was a remarkable leader, presiding over a time of growth, progress, and conflict. His pastorate (1866–1900) witnessed Reconstruction, the genesis of educational and financial institutions that would significantly serve the Black community, the resurgence of White conservative control, and the endangerment of all the political, economic, and social gains achieved since the end of slavery.

Dr. William Thomas Johnson was elected pastor, and his tenure of office (1901–1942) encompassed the Virginia Constitution of 1902, the Richmond Streetcar Boycott, two world wars, and the rise to power of the segregationist "Byrd Machine." The church grew in tandem with the Jackson Ward Community and Black institutions/businesses such as St. Luke's Penny Savings Bank, the Hippodrome Theatre, Slaughter's and Eggleston's Hotels, Armstrong and Maggie Walker High Schools, and Virginia Union University. In 1954, the same year that the Supreme Court decision in the *Brown v. Board of Education* case triggered the civil rights movement, First African Baptist Church began moving into the former Barton Heights Baptist Church at 2700 Hanes Avenue. The migration of Black families from the downtown sector to the north side of the city necessitated the church's relocation in order to better serve its constituency. Shortly after this move, Jackson Ward was devastated, and the adjoining Navy Hill sector of the city was virtually destroyed by the politically motivated routing of Interstate 95, resulting in the razing of hundreds of homes and businesses. The Richmond Coliseum Project further advanced this process. But First African Baptist Church persevered through tumultuous years that saw school desegregation; "massive resistance" by the Byrd Machine; the founding of the Richmond Crusade for Voters; the arrest of the Richmond 34 during the February 22, 1960, sit-in; and the Campaign for Human Dignity against the Jim Crow system in Richmond. Two civil rights attorneys who had worshiped at First African, L. Douglas Wilder and Roland J. Ealey, were elected to state office; the annexation and busing controversies raged; and a Black-majority city council, with Henry L. Marsh III as Richmond's first African American mayor, was elected in 1977. A succession of able ministers— Dr. Alexander L. James (1943–1946), Dr. Y.B. Williams (1948–1974), Don J. Hayes (1976–1986), Cessar L. Scott (1986–1987), Dr. Dennis E. Thomas (1987–2007), and Dr. Rodney D. Waller (2008–)—have piloted the church through many daunting challenges. Richmond remains in many ways a captive to its past. Issues of urban decay, unemployment and homelessness, crime, poverty, transportation, police-community relations, and economic viability frame an ever-present reality. First African has seen struggles continue through the COVID-19 crisis and the Black Lives Matter (BLM) protests of 2020. The George Floyd murder ignited demonstrations throughout Richmond from May 29 to August 16, 2020, and nearly every Confederate statue or memorial was removed. Through all, First African Baptist Church has continued its dedication to community service, the Christian gospel, and its mission of social justice.

One

IN THE SHADOW OF SLAVERY

1780–1865

The capital city of Richmond and First Baptist Church in effect grew up together. But for the city, the ever-present reality beneath the prestige offered by being the seat of state government and sporting such notable buildings as the Capitol, designed by Thomas Jefferson; Monumental Church; St. Paul's Episcopal Church; and St. Peter's Catholic Church was far from glamorous. The city of John Marshall, Edgar Allen Poe, and George Wythe was also the city of a large slave underclass, human trafficking on a massive scale, and businesses such as Lumpkin's and Omohundro's capitalizing on human misery with their slave prisons, auction houses, and whipping posts. But steadily and usually unobtrusively, the African American population—both freedmen and slaves—were making an impact and carving inroads to improve their situation. In 1841, they, at last, won the freedom to worship in their own church—First African Baptist, albeit with strings attached. The first pastor, Dr. Robert Ryland, though he was a slave owner himself and condoned slavery as an institution, nonetheless gave his Black deacons leeway to unofficially preach and ignored violations of the more odious racial laws of Virginia. Then, the cataclysmic events of 1861–1865 upended the old order of society as the Southern Confederacy struggled with the United States in the bloodiest war of the nation's history. On April 3, 1865, Union soldiers captured Richmond, the Confederate capital, and the Civil War would soon be over. Slavery was doomed, the Union was restored, and First African Baptist Church was now ready to move out of the shadow of slavery into a new era.

PINK AND CARRINGTON STREET CORNER, RICHMOND, VIRGINIA, 1956 (ABOVE) AND 2022 (BELOW).
As humble and unprepossessing as it was some 176 years earlier when First Baptist held services in a private house there, the corner of Pink and Carrington Streets in Richmond's East End was the worse for wear when these photographs were taken. For those who professed the Baptist faith in Virginia, persecution, imprisonment, and discrimination was a recent memory. The Virginia Statute for Religious Freedom had only been introduced in 1779 and would not be enacted into law until January 16, 1786. It was, therefore, prudent to tread softly because the dominant Episcopal Church was still very powerful. But in a few short years, the Baptist population would grow rapidly among both Black and White Richmonders. (Above, VHR; below, Dr. Kimberly A. Matthews.)

ST. JOHN'S EPISCOPAL CHURCH. As the oldest continuing church in Richmond, which was founded in 1741, and whose congregation includes most of the Anglican/Episcopalian elite, St. John's Episcopal Church long dominated its Baptist neighbors. But that would soon change, as First Baptist Church's membership soared and it became a power to be reckoned with by the early 19th century. There is a supreme irony in the fact that St. John's, which was the site for Patrick Henry's "Liberty or Death" speech on March 23, 1775, had many slaveholders, including Henry himself. (Both, LOC.)

HAITIAN REVOLUTION. On August 21, 1791, slaves in the French colony of Haiti, on the Caribbean island of Hispaniola, rose up against their plantation masters and waged a long and ultimately successful campaign for freedom. The leaders of the revolution, Toussaint L'Ouverture (in portrait) and Jean-Jacques Dessalines, proved to be extraordinary generals, and on January 1, 1804, Haiti became the second nation in the western hemisphere to secure its independence. In the Southern states, including Virginia, the Haitian Revolution was viewed with alarm, and there was fear that its continued success would inspire similar uprisings in the United States. This would indeed prove to be the case. (Left, HDHR; below, LOC.)

GABRIEL'S UPRISING, 1800. There exists no contemporary visual depiction of the slave Gabriel Prosser; the image here is based on conjecture. It is known that he was a blacksmith and the slave of the tobacco planter Thomas Prosser of Brookfield, Henrico County. Spurred on by events in Haiti, Prosser organized hundreds of Blacks in a plot to seize control of the state government and hold Gov. James Monroe hostage to negotiate for independence. A severe thunderstorm on August 30, 1800, delayed the scheduled uprising. The plot was betrayed the following day, and the authorities moved in to arrest the leaders. Prosser himself escaped from Richmond and fled to Norfolk. (Right, Jerome W. Jones Jr., HDHR; below, VDHR.)

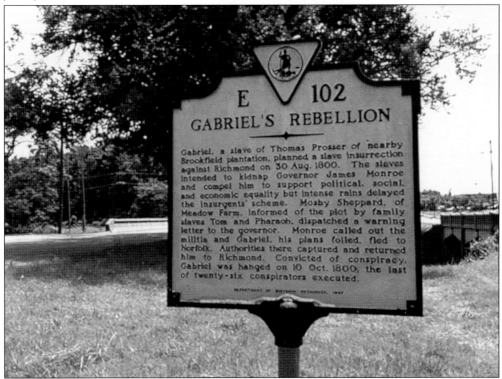

E 102
GABRIEL'S REBELLION

Gabriel, a slave of Thomas Prosser of nearby Brookfield plantation, planned a slave insurrection against Richmond on 30 Aug. 1800. The slaves intended to kidnap Governor James Monroe and compel him to support political, social, and economic equality but intense rains delayed the insurgents' scheme. Mosby Sheppard, of Meadow Farm, informed of the plot by family slaves Tom and Pharaoh, dispatched a warning letter to the governor. Monroe called out the militia and Gabriel, his plans foiled, fled to Norfolk. Authorities there captured and returned him to Richmond. Convicted of conspiracy, Gabriel was hanged on 10 Oct. 1800, the last of twenty-six conspirators executed.

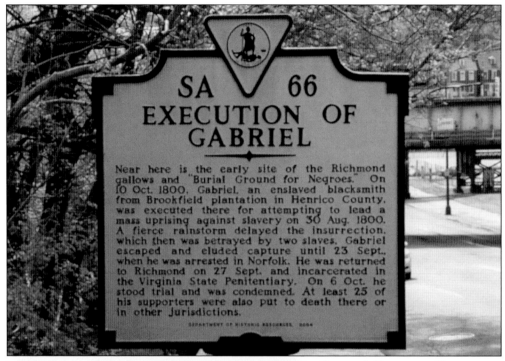

GABRIEL'S EXECUTION PLAQUE (ABOVE) AND THE SLAVE BURIAL GROUND (LEFT). Gabriel Prosser was apprehended in Norfolk on September 14, 1800, taken back to Richmond for trial, sentenced to death, and hanged on October 10, 1800, along with, in all, 26 fellow conspirators. The remnants of the gallows at the old Slave Burial Ground near Fifteenth and Broad Streets was probably the one on which Prosser was placed. Though the location of Prosser's grave is unrecorded, it was likely in the old African Burial Ground at Shockoe Bottom, where an unknown number of slaves were laid to rest in unmarked graves. On August 30, 2007, Virginia governor Tim Kaine articulated a pardon for Gabriel Prosser and the other participants. (Above, VDHR; left, Dr. Kimberly A. Matthews.)

The BURNING of the THEATRE in RICHMOND, VIRGINIA, on the Night of the 26ᵗʰ December 1811,
By which awful Calamity upwards of ONE HUNDRED of its most valuable Citizens suddenly lost their lives and many others were much injured.

Published Feb 18ᵗʰ 1812 by B. Tanner Nᵒ 74 South 8ᵗʰ St Philadelphia.

THE RICHMOND THEATRE FIRE. It was supposed to be a night for festive entertainment and socializing for Richmond's elite, including newly inaugurated governor George William Smith, at the Richmond Theatre on Broad Street, less than a block from First Baptist Church, on December 26, 1811. After the first act, a fire broke out, caused by a lighted chandelier, and spread rapidly. In the ensuing panic, 72 people were burned or trampled to death, including Governor Smith. It was Richmond's most horrific disaster up to that date, and the death toll would have been even higher if a hero had not rushed to the scene. (LOC.)

THE HEROIC BLACKSMITH GILBERT HUNT. Gilbert Hunt (1780?–1863), a slave who worked as a blacksmith and attended First Baptist, lived a few blocks away from the theater and ran to help when he heard about the fire. He stationed himself below a second-story window where he spotted Dr. James D. McCaw, a Richmond physician. Between them, McCaw and Hunt rescued 12 women, with McCaw lowering them from the window and Hunt—whose strength was said to be prodigious— catching them. McCaw finally had to jump to escape the flames and badly injured his leg. Hunt carried the doctor away to safety just before the wall was about to collapse on him. Hunt later bought his freedom and, in 1840, became a deacon at First African Baptist Church. (LOC.)

MONUMENTAL CHURCH. In the wake of the Richmond Theatre tragedy, a campaign was begun, led by Supreme Court chief justice John Marshall, to commission the famous Charleston architect, Robert Mills, to design a church to commemorate and house the ashes of the victims. In 1814, the structure, Monumental Episcopal Church, was completed in the Greek Revival style. A crypt below the church holds the remains of those who perished. Gilbert Hunt was (eventually) not forgotten; in 1931, a bronze plaque was affixed to the front wall of the church memorializing his heroic role, and a state historical marker mentioning him was erected in 1992 at the site. (Both, LOC.)

REV. LOTT CARY
A missionary to Africa.

LOTT CAREY (LEFT) AND HIS MISSION. A slave on the plantation of John Bowry in Charles City County, Lott Carey (1780–1828) was fortunate enough to be hired out by his master to work in Richmond at the Shockoe Tobacco Warehouse. He was baptized as a member of the First Baptist congregation in 1807 and bought his and his family's freedom by 1813. By then he had become a preacher of some note and in 1815 was a founder of the Richmond African Baptist Missionary Society, which sought to repatriate former slaves to Africa, and would merge its efforts with those of the American Colonization Society. On January 23, 1821, he sailed from Norfolk for West Africa. As a founding father of the colony (later Republic) of Liberia, he helped establish its capital of Monrovia, where he served as minister of Providence Baptist Church and vice agent of Liberia. An accidental gunpowder explosion led to his death in Monrovia on November 10, 1828. (Both, FABC).

Discovery of Nat Turner—wood engraving illustrating Benjamin Phipps's capture of Nat Turner

Library of Congress

NAT TURNER'S REVOLT AND ITS IMPACT. No slave uprising in the South resonated more forcefully than that led by the slave preacher Nat Turner in Southampton County from August 21 to October 10, 1831. Believing that God had spoken to him in a thunderstorm, Turner became convinced that he had a commission to lead an uprising to overthrow slavery. Organizing a small group of followers, he struck in the morning of August 21, 1831, and by August 23, his growing army advanced to the Southampton County seat of Jerusalem (now Courtland), where he was defeated by state militia and his followers scattered. Turner himself eluded capture until October 10 and was hanged on November 11, 1831. As a result of the uprising, Blacks throughout the South were massacred, and Virginia passed increasingly repressive legislation against both slaves and freedmen. (Above, LOC; below, HDHR.)

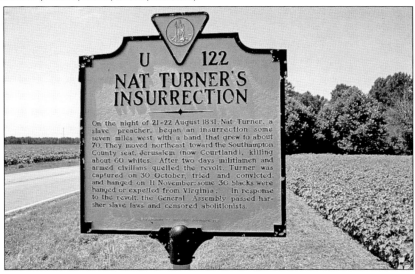

19

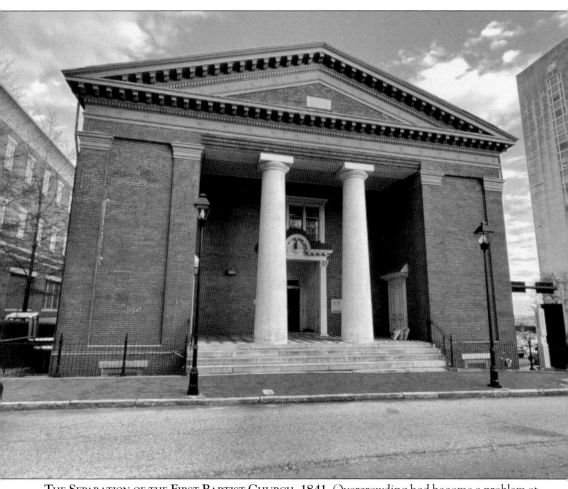

THE SEPARATION OF THE FIRST BAPTIST CHURCH, 1841. Overcrowding had become a problem at First Baptist, so it was decided to divide the congregation with the 387 White members moving into new premises near Twelfth and Broad Streets. The new building was designed at the cost of $40,000 in Greek Revival style by architect Thomas Ustick Walter, who also designed the dome for the US Capitol and Tabb Street Presbyterian Church in Petersburg, Virginia. The 1,708 Black members were allotted the old building (depicted above as it appears today) for the sum of $6,500, most of which was raised by subscription of the members themselves, and on October 1, 1841, First African Baptist Church was established as an individual entity. (Dr. Kimberly A. Matthews.)

Dr. Robert Ryland (Right) and Richmond College (Below). But separate existence did not yet translate to complete independence. Under the strictures put into law in the wake of Nat Turner's revolt, the congregation had to be shepherded by a White pastor; the first of these was Dr. Robert Ryland (1805–1899). Ryland also served as president of Richmond College on Grace Street (which developed into the University of Richmond) from 1841 to 1866. Ryland is a paradoxical figure who believed in slavery as a necessary step for the Christianization of African Americans (preaching that slaves should "obey their masters") but turned a blind eye to evasions of the restrictive laws and allowed the congregation considerable autonomy. He would also play a role in the establishment of Richmond Theological School for Freedmen (eventually Virginia Union University). (Right, Boatwright Library, University of Richmond; below, LOC.)

THE RESURRECTION OF HENRY BOX BROWN AT PHILADELPHIA.
Who escaped from Richmond Va. in a Box 3 feet long 2½ ft deep and 2 ft wide

HENRY "BOX" BROWN. Henry Brown, a slave from Louisa County, was sent to Richmond in 1830 to work in a tobacco factory, was baptized, and attended First African, singing in the choir. Angered at the shabby treatment he had received from his wife's master, who had promised not to sell her but instead betrayed him by selling her and their three children to a North Carolina plantation, Brown plotted a daring escape. Two friends, James Smith and Samuel Smith, packed him into a wooden crate and mailed him off to the Pennsylvania Anti-Slavery Society in Philadelphia on March 23, 1849, and after a harrowing journey by rail and cart, he was released from the crate the next day. His audacious act electrified the abolitionist movement. As Henry "Box" Brown, he achieved international celebrity as an author, magician, and activist. (Both, LOC.)

ANTHONY BURNS, PART I. Anthony Burns, a Virginia slave, was not as fortunate as Henry Brown. He did manage to escape from Richmond by sneaking on board a cargo ship but was recognized in Boston and imprisoned under the Fugitive Slave Act of 1850. A mob unsuccessfully tried to free him, and he was taken back to Richmond where, for four months, he was shackled and endured such brutal treatment, isolation, and derivation in Lumpkin's jail that his health was jeopardized. His master then sold him to the slave dealer David McDaniel in Rocky Mount, North Carolina. However, that was not the end. The outcome of Burns's story is revealed on page 33. (Both, LOC.)

23

THE FALL OF RICHMOND, Vᴬ ON THE NIGHT OF APRIL 2ᴰ 1865.

This strong hold the Capital City of the Confederacy, was evacuated by the Rebels in consequence of the defeat at 'Five Forks' of the Army of Northern Virginia under Lee, and capture of the South side Rail-Road by Genᶥ Grant .. Before abandoning the City, the Rebels set fire to it, destroying a vast amount of property and the conflagration continued until it was subdued by the Union troops on the following morning.

RICHMOND AND THE COMING OF WAR. As the seven deep Southern states seceded from the Union and began the Civil War against the United States by firing on Fort Sumter on April 12, 1861, Virginia was faced with a choice. The outcome was not a foregone conclusion; in the Virginia Convention of 1861, which met at the House of Delegates room of the Virginia State Capitol, there was a strong anti-secessionist sentiment among representatives of the western counties. However, the vote on April 16, 1861, was 88-55 in favor of joining the Southern Confederacy, and on May 20, 1861, Richmond became the Confederate capital, until the evacuation fire (depicted above) of April 2, 1865. (LOC.)

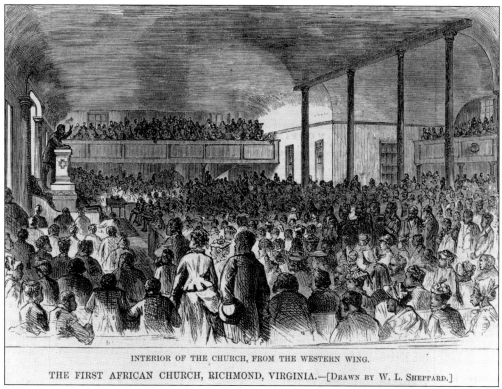

INTERIOR OF THE CHURCH, FROM THE WESTERN WING.

THE FIRST AFRICAN CHURCH, RICHMOND, VIRGINIA.—[Drawn by W. L. Sheppard.]

First African's Ironic Wartime Role and Judah P. Benjamin. First African Baptist Church sported one of Richmond's largest indoor meeting spaces. A contemporary account described it as "cavernous," as evidenced in this interior view. As such, the building was sometimes used for purposes far removed from worship—and sometimes even for segregated events. One of the oddest, unsegregated, events happened late in the war (March 1865) when Judah P. Benjamin (right), one of Confederate president Jefferson Davis's closest advisors, spoke at First African in order to recruit Black soldiers into the Confederate army. The Confederate congress had just passed a bill authorizing this as a desperation measure. A few were recruited (though it is not known if any were on this particular occasion), but the Confederacy fell soon afterward, and they never saw combat. (Above, FABC; right, LOC.)

ABRAHAM LINCOLN AND THE EMANCIPATION PROCLAMATION. Abraham Lincoln's philosophical evolution during the Jubilee War on the questions of slavery, Black military service, and African American citizenship rights is well-known. From insisting in 1861 on a "White man's war" and discounting that the abolition of slavery factored in the conflict, he had moved by the summer of 1862 to advocating emancipation and the admission of African Americans into the US armed forces. Timing the announcement to coincide with the turning back of the Confederate invasion of Maryland at the Battle of Antietam, Lincoln revealed the Emancipation Proclamation, which, as of January 1, 1863, declared all slaves in Confederate territory—including Richmond—to be "forever free." (LOC.)

ELIZABETH VAN LEW (RIGHT) AND
ELIZABETH DRAPER MITCHELL (BELOW).
They allegedly called the 45-year-old
spinster "Crazy Bet" because of her supposed
eccentricities. In reality, Elizabeth Van
Lew was a brilliant Union spymaster and
organized the highly effective Richmond
Underground espionage network from her
home in Church Hill. Most of her agents
were African American women, including
perhaps Elizabeth Draper Mitchell, mother
of Maggie Lena Walker, and Mary Bowser,
also known as Mary Jane Richards. Bowser
even infiltrated the White House of the
Confederacy as a servant and used her
photographic memory to transmit crucial
military information back to Van Lew, who
had direct contact with Union general
Ulysses S. Grant. The mysterious Mary
Bowser disappears from the historical record
in 1867, and no accurate likeness is known
to exist of her, though she is probably
buried at Section G Plot 23 in Woodland
Cemetery. But much more would be heard
from Maggie Lena Walker. (Both, NPS.)

THE LIBERATION AND BURNING OF RICHMOND. On April 2, 1865, General Grant captured the city of Petersburg, making the fall of Richmond inevitable. The Confederate government and army fled their capital, and Confederate general Richard S. Ewell ordered his men to set fire to tobacco and liquor warehouses. However, the wind blew the fire out of control and it caused pandemonium and looting, incinerating 30 city blocks. The next morning, Union troops marched in to liberate the city and assist in controlling the blaze. The evacuation fire did not come near First African Baptist Church, but for its congregants, this was undoubtedly a night of fear and hope. Change was coming. (Both, LOC.)

BLACK SOLDIERS, ARMY OF THE JAMES. The Emancipation Proclamation brought about a flood of enlistments from African Americans, both slave and free, eager to participate in restoring the Union and bringing about abolition. Some 200,000 are estimated to have joined, and these soldiers factored significantly in the ultimate Union victory. Most of the Black soldiers in Virginia were deployed to the east of Richmond in the Army of the James and had already proved their mettle in defeating Confederate forces at the hard-fought battle of New Market Heights in Henrico County on September 29, 1864. On April 3, 1865, Black troops from the 25th Corps of the Army of the James were among the first to enter Richmond, amidst cheers from African American residents who lined the streets. (LOC.)

GLIMPSES AT THE FREEDMEN—THE FREEDMEN'S UNION INDUSTRIAL SCHOOL, RICHMOND, VA.—FROM A SKETCH BY OUR SPECIAL ARTIST, JAS. E. TAYLOR.

THE FREEDMEN'S BUREAU (ABOVE) AND EDUCATION FOR FORMER SLAVES (BELOW). Though he had shortcomings, Pastor Ryland was firm in advocating education for African Americans in his congregation, especially in biblical studies. Education was also recognized as crucial if the benefits of newly won rights and freedom were to be fully realized after centuries of slavery and illiteracy. Among the organizations that stepped in to try to breach the knowledge gap were the American Baptist Home Mission Society (ABHMS) and the Freedmen's Bureau (Bureau of Refugees, Freedmen, and Abandoned Lands). As a federal agency, the bureau established several schools of varied emphases (ranging from trade schools to elementary schools, as per the images on this page). But more needed to be done to advance this effort, and First African Baptist Church would play its role in this. (Both, LOC.)

Two

IN THE ERA OF

JAMES HENRY HOLMES

1865–1900

Thanks to the events of early 1865, the old Richmond and the old First African Baptist Church were gone forever, and the new order quickly asserted itself. Juneteenth and the 13th Amendment to the Constitution would drive the final nails into slavery's coffin. Union soldiers arrived at First African and wanted to depose Dr. Ryland as pastor immediately, but the congregation came to his defense and spared him the indignity of being tossed out by voting to allow him to stay a little longer. Ryland would, however, resign on July 1, 1865, and was succeeded by the abolitionist Dr. George S. Stockwell, who was, in turn, followed in 1866 by James Henry Holmes, a former slave and the first African American minister. Pastor Holmes, who was to preside for 34 years, had led a remarkable life. Baptized in First African Baptist Church in 1846, he had suffered imprisonment for his part in assisting his father and mother-in-law in escaping to freedom, being separated from his family by being sold to Louisiana, and barely survived an explosion that gave him a concussion and severely injured his arm. Then his fortunes changed when he was sold again and returned to Richmond and First African in 1852, where he was elected as a deacon. During his pastorate, Holmes presided over the construction of a new church building in 1876 and was one of the earliest students to matriculate at Richmond Theological School for Freedmen, present-day Virginia Union University. During his time at the school, Holmes and his family resided at the Lumpkin's Jail campus. Thereafter, he played a major role in the school's progress, being among the first African Americans to serve on its board of trustees. Guiding both his church and the theological school through the years of Reconstruction, and the White backlash that followed it, Holmes would be conferred with an honorary doctorate by Shaw University. Dr. Holmes lived to see the formal establishment of Virginia Union University in 1899 and died on November 26, 1900.

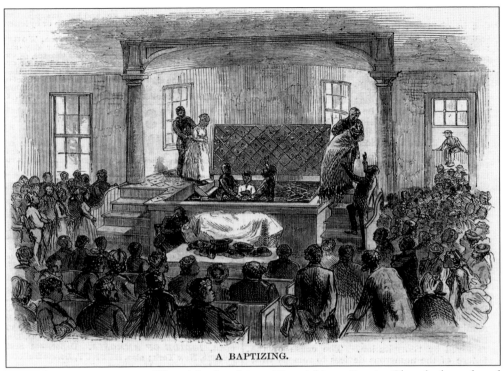

A BAPTIZING.

FIRST AFRICAN AFTER THE WAR. Membership at First African Baptist Church skyrocketed dramatically during and just after the war. Baptisms, such as those pictured above in *Harper's Weekly*, accelerated in their frequency and continued to do so through the immediate postwar years. Ryland's continued pastorate was problematic, and though the congregation voted to retain him despite the urging of Union troops that he be dismissed, he resigned on July 1, 1865. His successor was a Northern abolitionist minister, Dr. George S. Stockwell, whose prior role in the rescue of Anthony Burns is related on page 33. (Both, FABC.)

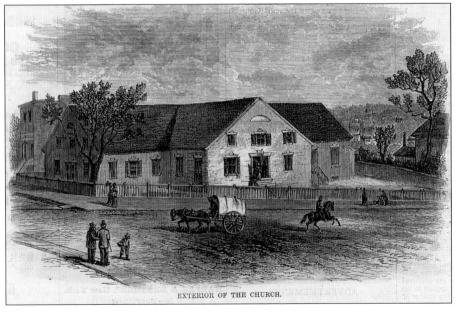

EXTERIOR OF THE CHURCH.

ANTHONY BURNS, PART II. In 1855, Dr. George S. Stockwell was in Amherst, Massachusetts, when he chanced to hear that the re-enslaved Anthony Burns (see page 25) was in Rocky Mount, North Carolina. He wrote to Burns's master, David McDaniel, who agreed to sell Burns for $1,325. Stockwell collaborated with fellow abolitionist Leonard Grimes to raise the money, and Burns was freed on February 27, 1855. Burns went on a speaking tour and became the pastor of St. Catherine's Baptist Church of Ontario, Canada, where he died July 27, 1862, from tuberculosis. The indignation over his earlier treatment, as evidenced in the poster, contributed to growing Northern antislavery sentiment. (Right, LOC; below, Boston Public Library.)

Dr. James Henry Holmes. First African's transformative pastor, James Henry Holmes (1826–1900), was born into slavery in rural King & Queen County, Virginia. At the age of 11, he was leased out by his master to Richmond tobacco manufacturer Samuel Meyers. He was baptized by Dr. Robert Ryland into the First African congregation in 1842 and married in 1846. Two years later, he was accused of plotting the escape of his father-in-law, John Smith, and his own potential escape on the Underground Railroad, incarcerated in Omohundro's slave prison and sold to labor in the harbor of New Orleans, where he was nearly killed by a boiler explosion. Recovering, he was resold, and his new master took him back to Richmond. He was named deacon at First African in 1855 and officially elected pastor in 1867. (VUU.)

Dr. Nathaniel Colver. Dr. Nathaniel Colver (1794–1870) from Orwell, Vermont, became a Baptist minister and an outspoken abolitionist. In 1867, at the age of 73, he was charged with reviving an educational institution for former slaves in Richmond, Virginia. It was originally called Richmond Theological School for Freedmen, and he secured the former site of Robert Lumpkin's slave trading complex as its campus. Colver presided over its operations and taught classes in tandem with Robert Ryland from 1867 to 1868. They made a bizarre combination: Ryland had spoken in the past in support of slavery as a necessity for the Christianization of African Americans, and Colver saw it as an unmitigated moral evil. However, it seemed to function. Colver retired because of failing health and died on December 25, 1870. (VUU.)

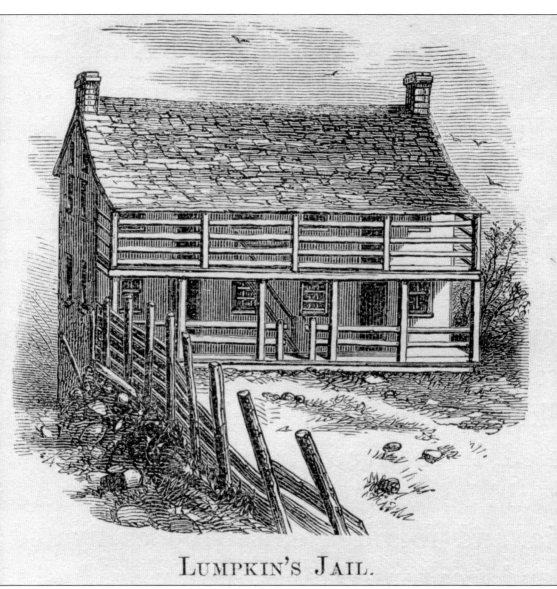

Lumpkin's Jail.

Lumpkin's Jail Campus. The despised slave prison and complex known as "the Devil's Half Acre," owned by Robert Lumpkin, had a redemptive postbellum life when it served for three years (1867–1870) as the venue for Richmond Theological School for Freedmen and was rechristened "God's Half Acre." During this time, Mary F. Lumpkin, the late owner's widow and a congregant at First African, leased the complex to the American Baptist Home Mission Society for $1,000 per year, and Pastor James Henry Holmes resided there with his family, both as a student and as an assistant. One of the most endearing recollections was that of Dr. Holmes years later describing how Dr. Colver would sometimes take Holmes's toddler son out of the mud in which he had been playing and carry him around (VUU).

PASTOR JAMES HENRY HOLMES (ABOVE) AND THE SOLOMON MARABLE CASE. Pastor Holmes, respected during his lifetime as one of the foremost postwar African American leaders, effectively defined First African Church's place in the greater Richmond community and the principles it stood for. He administered the construction of a new church building in 1876 and helped bring about the establishment of Virginia Union University in 1899. Solomon Marable was a Black man executed (some say unjustly) for murder in 1896. His body was taken to Richmond and seized by the Anatomical Board of the Medical College of Virginia (MCV) for dissection. *Richmond Planet* editor John Mitchell Jr., a member of the FABC congregation, enlisted Dr. Holmes's help in successfully persuading MCV to release the body to Marable's widow, Fannie. In the image, Holmes is at the bottom right, calling upon MCV custodian Chris Baker. (Both, FABC.)

Rev. J. H. Holmes calling upon Chris Baker to give up the body of Marable. Revs. Graham, Gullins and Brice, may be seen viewing the situation.

THE 1876 BUILDING. The editor of *Harper's Weekly* condemned the dismantling of FABC's original structure and its replacement by a new church building as showing no "appreciation for old things," but Pastor Holmes and his congregation saw it as a necessity in view of FABC's tremendous growth; it was reputed by some to be among the largest churches in the United States at the time. The architect was Thomas Ustick Walter (see page 22). The church originally had a tall steeple, but this was later removed as a safety hazard, as were many other Richmond church steeples over the years. (FABC.)

ALBERT ROYAL BROOKS AND ROBERT PEEL BROOKS. Albert R. Brooks (c. 1817–1881, seated third from left) was one of the earliest Black businessmen in Richmond and a charter member of First African, serving on the Board of Deacons. He owned restaurants and livery stables and, by 1865, had become prominent enough to be selected as a juror in the proposed treason trial of former Confederate president Jefferson Davis. In the end, the government did not prosecute Davis, and he was released in 1867. Albert Brooks's son Robert Peel Brooks (1853–1882) became a lawyer, newspaper editor (the *Richmond Virginia Star*), and a Republican party activist. In 1880, he was elected secretary of the party's State Central Committee. Unfortunately, his life was cut short by typhoid fever on October 10, 1882. (Both, LOC.)

NEW YORK : SATURDAY, FEBRUARY 14, 1885.

THE LATE ROBERT PEEL BROOKS.

LUCY GOODE BROOKS (LEFT) AND THE COLORED ORPHAN ASYLUM (BELOW). Another member of the remarkable Brooks family was Lucy Goode Brooks (1818–1900), who joined FABC on November 11, 1838; married Albert Brooks on February 2, 1839; and was Robert Peel Brooks's mother. In 1867, she and Pastor Holmes began a collaborative effort with the Cedar Creek Society of Friends (Quaker) to establish the Friends' Asylum for Colored Orphans and raised funds for a building at the intersection of St. Paul and Charity Streets. It is now known as the Friends' Association for Children, located at 1004 St. John's Street. The Lucy Brooks Foundation, which helps finance its continued operations, was named for her in 1984. (Both, LOC.)

DEACON WILLIAM WHITE (RIGHT) AND "MAGGIE MITCHELL'S ALLEY" (BELOW) Maggie Lena Draper's mother had married William Mitchell in 1868, but he died in 1876, leaving his family impoverished and living in rental quarters in College Alley (below), a block from FABC. It became known colloquially as "Maggie Mitchell's Alley" because the little girl was always playing there and her mother frequently yelled "Maggie Mitchell!" at the top of her lungs. Deacon William White (right), the Sunday school superintendent at FABC walked by one day and noticed little Maggie playing in the alley. He invited her into the church to play with the other children there and in doing so changed her life and the course of Richmond's history. (Both, NPS.)

41

YOUNG MAGGIE MITCHELL WALKER AND HER BAPTISM. The little girl befriended by Deacon White proved to be a brilliant student and a fervent worshipper at FABC. It was during this time that a "Great Revival" movement spread across the South, and many individuals rushed to be baptized. One such mass baptism was conducted by Pastor Holmes in the James River since the baptistery at First African would have had difficulty accommodating the estimated 300–600 candidates Among those who were baptized that day was Maggie Mitchell, who would join the Order of St. Luke that same year (1878) and, in 1882, would marry Armstead Walker, a prosperous Richmond bricklayer. (NPS.)

Dr. Charles Henry Corey (Right) and the United States Hotel. The Lumpkin's Jail campus, while it served its purpose from 1867 to 1870, was not considered an ideal venue for a school for African Americans. Most of the students were former slaves, and the very surroundings of the former "Devil's Half Acre" undoubtedly brought unpleasant memories to mind. Therefore, when the Richmond Theological School for Freedmen, renamed Colver Institute in 1869, received $10,000 from the Freedmen's Bureau, school president Dr. Charles Henry Corey and the trustees immediately purchased the building that had been the former United States Hotel at Nineteenth and Main Streets. There it would remain, with Pastor Holmes as one of its trustees, until its merger with Wayland Seminary to form Virginia Union University in 1899 (Both, VUU.)

RICHMOND THEOLOGICAL SEMINARY.

Richmond Photo Co, 827½ Broad St. Richmond Va.

Dr. Lyman Beecher Tefft (Left) and Carrie Victoria Dyer (Below). Born in Exeter, Rhode Island, Tefft was an active abolitionist minister affiliated with the American Baptist Home Mission Society. Obtaining a doctorate in divinity from Brown University, Dr. Tefft was, in 1873, appointed principal of Nashville Normal and Theological Institute, an HBCU that specialized in training African American men for the ministry and women for the teaching profession. In 1883, he conceived, helped to establish, and served for 29 years as the first president of Richmond's Hartshorn Memorial College, which catered exclusively to African American women. He was assisted by Carrie Victoria Dyer, the college principal and later, dean. The curriculum was based on that of Wellesley College. (Both, VUU)

Richmond Photo Co. 827½ Broad St., RICHMOND, VA.

HARTSHORN MEMORIAL COLLEGE. Tefft's and Dyer's conception of women's education was quite advanced for its time, inculcating in the students the idea of preparation for assuming leadership or partnership roles with men rather than subordination. Many of the students became FABC congregants, and Maggie Walker served on the college board of trustees. Hartshorn merged into Virginia Union University in 1932, and its former campus on Leigh and Lombardy Streets became the site of Maggie Walker High School. (Above, VUU; right, VDHR.)

EBENEZER BAPTIST CHURCH. By 1855, less than 15 years after First African had separated from First Baptist, it was again confronted with the issue of overcrowded facilities, with membership soaring above 3,000 members. A "colony" of some 400, therefore, branched off and met at a building on a lot that had been purchased in Bacon Quarter Branch Creek at the corner of Judah and Leigh Streets on the North Side of the city. According to one account, the site was chosen when one of the members of the organizing committee, Benjamin Harris, had a vision of a man standing atop the surface of the creek at the site indicating that a church should be built there. The building was dedicated on April 4, 1858. The original name of Third Baptist Church was changed to Ebenezer. (Dr. Kimberly A. Matthews.)

Pastor John Jasper (Right) and Sixth Mount Zion Baptist Church (Below). One of the many offshoots of Richmond's First African "Mother Church" was Sixth Mount Zion Baptist Church, located in Jackson Ward at 14 West Duval Street. Its founding pastor, John Jasper, was a former slave from Fluvanna County, Virginia, and a member of First African. Jasper and his adherents branched off on September 3, 1867, and met in a horse stable on Brown's Island in the James River. In 1869, they moved to Duval Street, and the present structure (with modifications carried out in 1925) was built. In the late 1950s, the church was slated to be demolished to make way for Interstate 95 through Jackson Ward. Such an outcry of protest ensued, however, that the authorities relented and rerouted Interstate 95 around the rear of the church. (Right, LOC; below, the *Richmond Times-Dispatch*.)

Richmond Photo. Co.   827½ Broad St.

DR. JOSEPH ENDOM JONES (1852–1922). Joseph Endom Jones from Lynchburg, Virginia, was among the first students at Richmond Theological School for Freedmen, attending from 1868 to 1871. He was born into slavery but rapidly advanced after he had secured his freedom, ultimately earning a master of arts degree from Colgate University and a doctor of divinity from Selma University. He taught homiletics and philosophy at Virginia Union University for 46 years, from 1876 to 1922. Jones focused on developing leadership skills and a sense of social justice in his students, a quality he also imparted to his son, Eugene Kinckle Jones Sr. Jones Sr. became one of the founders ("jewels") of Alpha Phi Alpha Fraternity in 1906 while at Cornell University and secretary to the Urban League. (VUU.)

Dr. Malcolm MacVicar (1829–1904). Known as "that man of iron and steel" in reference to his formidable and tenacious personality, the Scottish-born Baptist minister Dr. Malcolm MacVicar held the post of secretary to the American Baptist Home Mission Society and, in close alliance with Dr. Holmes and Dr. Joseph Endom Jones, was instrumental in persuading the society to locate its prospective University for African Americans in Richmond rather than in Atlanta. When Wayland Seminary and Richmond Theological Seminary merged in 1899 to establish Virginia Union University, Dr. MacVicar was named its first president and served until his passing on May 17, 1904. (VUU.)

JUBAL EARLY (LEFT) AND THE UNITED DAUGHTERS OF THE CONFEDERACY (BELOW). Almost as soon as the dust had cleared after the Jubilee War, there were concerted efforts in the South to dismantle Reconstruction, glamorize the Confederacy, disfranchise African Americans, and generally undo the war's results. One key to this effort was the creation of the "Lost Cause" myth. The South was depicted as being noble and virtuous, and the evils of slavery were downplayed and denied. Former Confederate general Jubal Early, a White supremacist, played a major part in perpetuating these misrepresentations, directing the Southern Historical Society from 1873 to 1894, the year of his death. In that same year, the United Daughters of the Confederacy was founded and dedicated itself to fostering the Lost Cause in the schools and erecting monuments and memorials to Confederate figures. These efforts would also translate into the political realm. (Both, LOC.)

ERECTING THE LEE STATUE (RIGHT) AND THOMAS S. MARTIN (BELOW). The statue of Robert E. Lee, seen here being unveiled in 1890, was the first of the Confederate statues on Richmond's Monument Avenue, and the former Confederate capital would eventually be festooned with such monuments. More devastating was the establishment of a Conservative Democratic political machine that was founded by former Confederate veteran and US senator Thomas S. Martin (1847–1919) and continued into the 1960s by Sen. Harry F. Byrd Sr. The machine was dedicated to racial segregation and voter restriction and suppression, targeting African American and poorer White voters. Martin was the main architect of the 1902 Virginia Constitution, which locked in racial discrimination and cemented the dictatorial power of the machine "bosses." It was not superseded until 1971. (Right, VHC; below, LOV.)

BUILDING VIRGINIA UNION UNIVERSITY, 1899–1900. While Martin and his allies were consolidating their power, there was significant movement in an opposite direction as the new Virginia Union University emerged at North Lombardy Street as Virginia's first African American University. Nine structures, built of Virginia granite and Georgia pine and designed by the world-renowned architect John Hopper Coxhead, were constructed, beginning on February 11, 1899. Students themselves worked on their construction. The image above depicts Coburn Hall, the university chapel and library. The image below shows some of the students putting together Kingsley Hall, which served as the first student dormitory. It was the fulfillment of one of Pastor Holmes's culminating projects—in realization—where he and other First African congregants played an important role. (Both, VUU.)

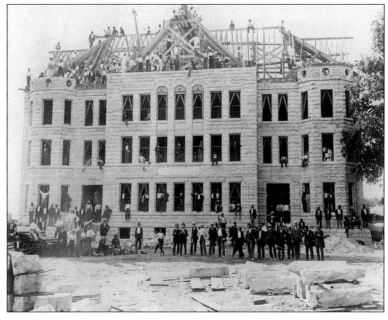

Three

In the
Early 20th Century
1900–1950

For First African Baptist Church, the new century, unfortunately, began with a bitterly contested pastoral election to determine Dr. Holmes's successor and a most vitriolic and divisive aftermath. On June 3, 1901, the election was held, and three candidates were considered: A.W. Pegues, William Thomas "W.T." Johnson, and W.H. Brooks. Johnson was elected, but the results were adamantly disputed by congregant John Mitchell Jr., the editor of the *Richmond Planet*. Mitchell was disfellowshipped on July 15, 1901, and Johnson was officially installed on August 5.

More disconcerting events were soon to follow. The so-called "progressive movement" of the first two decades of the 20th century did not live up to that label as far as the African American community was concerned. Instead, those years became known as the "nadir" of race relations in the United States and saw the reemergence of the Ku Klux Klan into a powerful force in national politics.

Despite obstacles, Pastor Johnson and his congregation persevered, buttressed by the presence of an exceptional financial mind and civic leader, Maggie Lena Walker. Johnson's years at the helm (1901–1942) were years of growth and consolidation and coincided with the heyday of Richmond's Jackson Ward enclave, which prospered to such an extent with a proliferation of Black-owned businesses that it was dubbed the "Black Wall Street" (a title it shared for a while with tragic Greenwood District of Tulsa, Oklahoma). Jackson Ward also earned the sobriquet "Harlem of the South" as a Southern haven for artists and performers of the Harlem Renaissance. After Dr. Johnson's passage, Dr. Alexander L. James pastored from 1943 to 1946. His successor, after an interim pastorate under Rev. David Fitzgerald, Dr. Y.B. (Yarborough Burrell) Williams, installed in 1948, confronted many challenges. The old building at College and Broad Streets was no longer meeting the needs of the congregation as efficiently as before—the majority of its members had moved north and west. Regarding the larger picture, the African American community in Virginia was becoming impatient over the continued dominance of Byrd Machine–sponsored segregation and discrimination. Pressure was mounting for change.

THE CAMPUS OF VIRGINIA UNION UNIVERSITY, C. 1907. When Virginia Union University was established and built at 1500 North Lombardy Street from 1899 to 1900, it was the most extensive construction project of its time in Virginia. Nine buildings (seven of which can be seen in this photograph) were designed by architect John Hopper Coxhead (1861–1943) and constructed, in

part by the students themselves, from Virginia granite and Georgia pine. The groundbreaking Founders' Day ceremony took place on February 11, 1899, and classes opened on October 4, 1899. It is not documented as to whether Pastor Holmes was present at these events, though, as a trustee board member, it is quite likely that he was. (LOC.)

IN MEMORY OF OUR PASTOR
REV. JAS H. HOLMES D.D.
BORN IN THE YEAR 1826.
DIED NOV. 25TH 1900.
LENGTH OF PASTORATE 34 YEARS.

DR. HOLMES'S PASSING AND THE STAINED-GLASS WINDOW. Dr. Holmes began suffering health issues and on October 7, 1900, it was announced that would retire as pastor emeritus on January 1, 1901, and be awarded $400 yearly for the remainder of his life in recognition for his exemplary service. This never came to pass as Pastor Holmes transitioned on November 25, 1900. According to a contemporary newspaper article, he was laid to rest in Ham Cemetery in Richmond's West End, but other sources indicate Barton Heights Cemetery, on the North Side. He was considered such a pivotal figure in the development and spiritual life of the church that a stained-glass window with his portrait was installed; it can be seen today at the church building on Hanes Avenue. (FABC.)

JOHN MITCHELL JR. (RIGHT) AND THE PASTORAL ELECTION CONTROVERSY. Known as the "Fighting Editor," John Mitchell Jr. (1863–1929) was born into slavery and first embarked on a career as a teacher before turning to journalism and social activism. As editor of the *Richmond Planet* from 1883 to 1929, he became renowned for his uncompromising editorials against lynching, segregation, and disfranchisement. His role as a congregant at First African, however, elicited a good bit of controversy within the Black community. His vehemence in opposing the election of Dr. William Thomas Johnson to the pastorate in succession to Dr. Holmes ended with his being disfellowshipped. (Right, LOV; below, LOC.)

Rev. W. T. Johnson, D. D.,
PASTOR FIRST BAPTIST CHURCH,
RICHMOND, VA.

DR. WILLIAM THOMAS JOHNSON (1866–1942). Regardless of the contentious nature of his election, Pastor Johnson proved an enduring and proactive pilot through the often treacherous early decades of the 20th century, a period sometimes called the "nadir" of American racial justice. His pastoral tenure, from 1901 to 1942, was the longest in the church's history and a most energetic and eventful one. Dr. Johnson brought the ladies into the forefront of directing church affairs by establishing the Deaconess Board and worked in tandem with Maggie Lena Walker and the St. Luke's Penny Savings Bank she founded (see page 68) on church and community projects and structural renovations to the church building. He passed on August 28, 1942. (FABC.)

THE RICHMOND TROLLEY BOYCOTT OF 1904. Although "Jim Crowism," racial separation, and second-class citizenry were the rule rather than the exception in early-20th-century Virginia—Richmond included—this was not meekly accepted, and there was some pushback. Richmond was the first city in the South to run a public streetcar transportation service (1888), and for 16 years, it was mainly integrated. But in 1904, Virginia General Assembly legislation gave transport companies the right to decide on whether to segregate or not and gave conductors the power to move and even arrest passengers who would not comply. Virginia Passenger and Power Company ran Richmond's trolleys and decided on segregation. On April 17, 1904, John Mitchell Jr. wrote a scathing indictment of this policy in the *Richmond Planet*, and at a mass meeting two days later, a complete boycott of all streetcars by the African American community was announced. The boycott succeeded in the short term when the company was consequently forced into bankruptcy, but in 1906, the General Assembly passed a law mandating transport segregation. (Both, LOC.)

EMANCIPATION DAY PARADE. Far from being forgotten, the liberation of Richmond on April 3, 1865, was celebrated by members of the African American community for years afterward as Emancipation Day. This image depicts the Emancipation Day parade of April 3, 1905, as it moved past the corner of Main and Tenth Streets. This was in spite and defiance of the flurry of discriminatory legislation that marked the politics of turn-of-the-century Virginia. (LOC.)

Eva Roberta Coles Boone. The Boone family was closely tied to First African and its missionary endeavors in Africa. Dr. Clinton Caldwell Boone and his first wife, Eva Roberta Coles (1880–1902), were the first missionaries sent out to Africa by the Lott Carey Foreign Mission Convention. She is also pictured below, seated second from left, with her 1899 graduating class from Hartshorn Memorial College. She then taught in her hometown of Charlottesville, Virginia, and, in 1901, married Clinton Boone, a 1900 graduate of Virginia Union University. The Boones were assigned to the mission station at Palabala in what became the Democratic Republic of the Congo. She taught kindergarten, started a sewing circle for women, and gained the respect and trust of those in her charge but sadly died of a poisoned bite on December 8, 1902. (Both, VUU.)

RACHEL ALLEN THARPS BOONE. After the untimely death of his wife, Eva, in the Congo, Clinton Boone returned to the United States in 1906 and went to medical school, ultimately earning degrees in both medicine (Shaw University, 1910) and dentistry (Bodee Dental School, 1919). In 1919, he remarried Rachel Allen Tharps, whose family members were active communicants at First African. From 1920 to 1926, Clinton and Rachel Boone were stationed as missionaries in Liberia, where their two children were born. Clinton authored two books about his missionary experiences: *Congo As I Knew It* (1927) and *Liberia As I Saw It* (1929). His family settled in Richmond at Navy Hill. Rachel died of tuberculosis on February 24, 1938, and Clinton drowned in the James River near Jamestown on July 2, 1939. (VUU.)

DR. BESSIE BEATRICE THARPS (1886–1979). Bessie Tharps, described as "one of the nation's pioneer Black female physicians," graduated from Hartshorn Memorial College (1912) and earned her doctor of medicine at Boston University (1916). She was reputed to be the second female African American practitioner in Richmond, after Sarah Boyd Jones. She served on FABC's Deaconess Board and was active in the East End Auxiliary, the Church Aid Society, and the Pastor's Aid Group. She specialized in obstetrics, homeopathy, and anesthesiology and, in addition to her private practice, worked at the Janice Porter Barret School in Hanover, Virginia, and later at Nannie Burroughs School in Washington, DC. (NPS.)

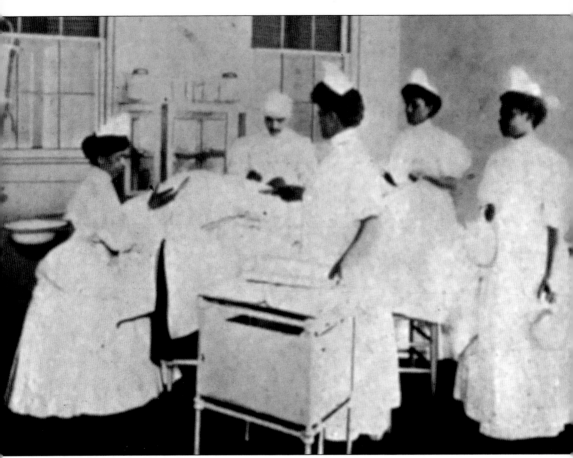

THE 1918 INFLUENZA PANDEMIC. Like everywhere else, the 1918 influenza pandemic hit the Richmond area hard. In Virginia, the death toll was nearly 16,000 out of over 325,000 cases by the time the pandemic ran its course in 1919—at least 1,069 deaths occurred in Richmond. It is of significance that, regardless of the emergency, the laws of racial segregation were nonetheless maintained. Even though doctors and nurses of all races were readily accepted into service, both patients and practitioners were rigidly separated. African American patients were placed in emergency facilities at Baker Elementary School, located in Jackson Ward on Baker and Charity Streets. Dr. Bessie Tharps served there as the assistant head physician under Dr. William Henry Hughes, who was also Maggie Walker's family physician. (LOC.)

THE KU KLUX KLAN PARADE THROUGH RICHMOND, 1920. The 1920s saw the revived Ku Klux Klan at its highest level of political power and influence. Resuscitated during the Wilson administration through the release of the Hollywood blockbuster film *Birth of a Nation* and gaining unprecedented support in Northern states from the slogan "100% Americanism," Klan members would openly and even routinely march and demonstrate through city streets in their "shrouds," as they dubbed their robes and hoods. The image depicts one such march through downtown Richmond in 1920. A massive rally through Washington, DC, down Pennsylvania Avenue in 1925 is estimated to have involved 35,000 marchers. (VHC.)

"Eugenics" Advocate Walter Plecker. One of the most fanatical proponents of the then trendy eugenics, or "racial science," movement that fostered White supremacy, Walter Ashby Plecker (1861–1947) was originally a medical practitioner who graduated from medical school at the University of Maryland and became notorious for his role in drafting the Virginia Racial Integrity Act of 1924, one of several such pieces of legislation that the Nazis drew inspiration from in enacting the infamous Nuremberg Laws of 1935. As the registrar for the Virginia Department of Vital Statistics from 1912 to 1946, Plecker denied the existence of Native American nations by designating them as "colored." The Virginia Racial Integrity Act outlawed interracial marriages and was not done away with until declared unconstitutional in the case of *Loving v. Virginia* (1967). (The *Richmond Times-Dispatch*.)

SEN. HARRY F. BYRD SR. Harry Flood Byrd Sr. (1887–1966) took over the conservative Democratic political organization founded by Thomas S. Martin and ran it with a tight grip from 1926 to 1963, when his control began to unravel under pressure from the civil rights movement, increased urbanization, and changing Virginia demographics. As governor (1926–1930) and US senator (1933–1965), he endeavored to maintain Jim Crow laws, segregated schools, voter suppression, and a "pay as you go" fiscal policy. The Byrd Machine faced quiet but consistent opposition from the Black churches of Richmond, which encouraged and provided meeting space for organizations like the Southern Christian Leadership Conference and the Richmond Crusade for Voters. (VHC.)

Maggie Lena Walker (Left) and St. Luke's Penny Savings Bank (Below). Maggie Lena Walker considered Pastor James Holmes and Deacon William White to have been two of the greatest influences on her life. Walker's most significant achievement was to serve as the first woman bank president in the United States. She joined the Independent Order of St. Luke in 1878 and, in 1899, was elected to its top leadership position: right worthy grand secretary. In 1902, she established and became CEO of the St. Luke's Penny Savings Bank, which later became Consolidated Bank & Trust. With her husband, Armstead Walker, she purchased a home at 110 ½ East Leigh Street in Jackson Ward. (Both, NPS.)

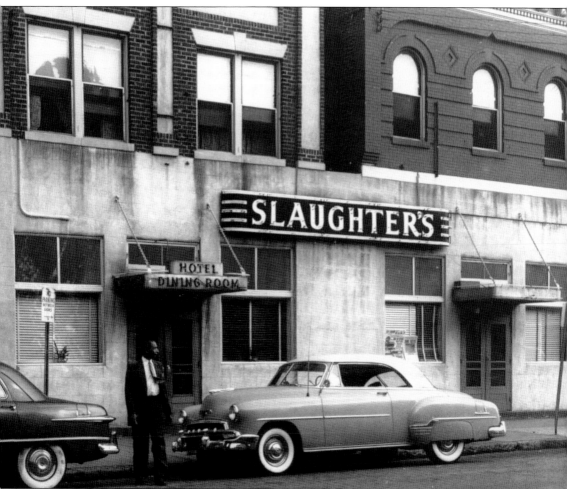

SLAUGHTER'S HOTEL IN JACKSON WARD. Second Street in Richmond's Jackson Ward was known far and wide as "the Deuce" and was the bustling center for nightlife, entertainment, the hospitality industry, and business for the Black community. Slaughter's Hotel was one of the meccas for celebrities from the entertainment, commercial, and artistic world when they would journey and stay in Richmond and, of course, a mainstay of the local economy. Nearly all of the businesses were Black-owned and family-owned. Nearby Eggleston Hotel, which would figure significantly in the civil rights Campaign for Human Dignity in 1960, provided the main competition. (VUU.)

THE HIPPODROME THEATRE. During the years that Richmond's Jackson Ward community thrived and prospered, it was known as the "Harlem of the South." Nearly every celebrity artist and musician associated with the Harlem Renaissance would come to Richmond to perform on what was termed the "Chitlin' Circuit," as the theaters and clubs that catered specifically to African American entertainers and patrons were called. Foremost among the establishments that hosted these appearances was the Hippodrome Theatre on Second Street. Founded in 1914 and featuring stars like Louis Armstrong, Billie Holiday, Ella Fitzgerald, James Brown, and Bill Robinson, it was closed down on several occasions but has now been reopened as a theater. (Dr. Kimberly A. Matthews.)

DR. JOHN MALCUS ELLISON (1889–1979). The figure of Dr. John Malcus Ellison (1889–1979) continues to loom large over both First African and Virginia Union. Although he is not as well-known as he should be, his impact on the spiritual and educational life of Richmond's Black community has been immeasurable. As president of Virginia Union University from 1941 to 1955, he placed the institution on a firm financial footing, directed the campaign to bring the Belgian Pavilion from its site at the New York World's Fair to the VUU campus, and established the university's renowned Graduate School of Theology in 1942. Among the ministers of First African who have received their instruction and degrees from the school (now the Samuel Dewitt Proctor School of Theology) were Dr. Alexander James, Dr. Y.B. Williams, Dr. Rodney D. Waller, and Cessar A. Scott. (VUU.)

BILL "BOJANGLES" ROBINSON (LEFT) AND THE STATUE AT "BOJANGLES INTERSECTION" (BELOW). Bill (originally Luther) Robinson (1878–1949) grew up in Jackson Ward. His mother, Maria, directed the FABC choir but died when Robinson was six, as did his father, Maxwell. He first began his dancing career as a child, performing on Second Street in front of the Globe Theatre; during this time, for reasons unknown, he acquired the nickname "Bojangles." After serving in the Spanish-American War, he went into show business and ultimately became a Hollywood film celebrity and the highest-paid African American artist of the time. He later donated funds for the installation of traffic lights at the intersection of Leigh and Adams Streets in Jackson Ward, primarily for the safety of students at Armstrong High School nearby. In 1973, a statue of Robinson was erected there in his honor. (Left, NPS; below, Dr. Kimberly A. Matthews.)

MARGARET ROSE MICHIE JOHNSON (RIGHT) AND ROSA DIXON BOWSER (BELOW). As Pastor Johnson's wife, Margaret Rose Michie Johnson (1874–1947) played a crucial and active role, as did many ladies at FABC. Johnson brought the women into the forefront of church life and organization and founded and edited the first church bulletin for seven years. Besides Maggie Walker—who was actually the Johnsons' next-door neighbor on Leigh Street—there was Rosa Dixon Bowser (1855–1931), a noted educator and social reformer, who began her teaching career holding Sunday school classes at FABC. She went on to teach at Navy Hill and Baker Elementary. She helped found the Virginia State Teachers' Association and served as its president from 1890 to 1892. She was proactive in the effort to commute Virginia Christian's death sentence (page 74) and in the campaign to end lynching. (Right, FABC; below, NPS.)

Mrs. Rosa D. Bowser.

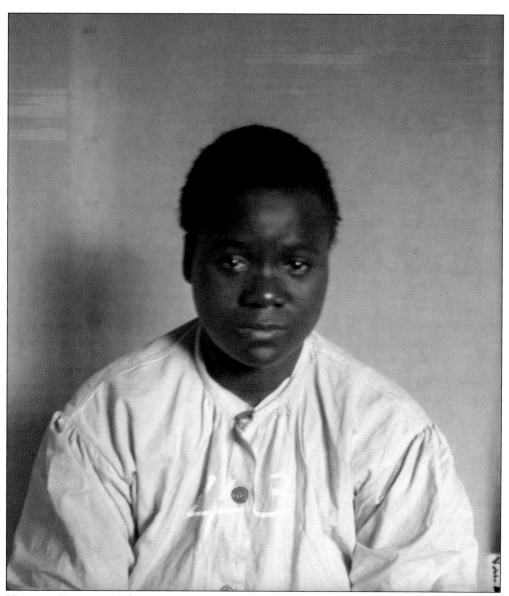

VIRGINIA CHRISTIAN. The unique circumstances surrounding the case of the 16-year-old laundry maid, Virginia Christian (1895–1912), galvanized activists like Rosa Dixon Bowser, Maggie Walker, and Mary Church Terrell and heightened awareness of racial discrepancies in the state's legal system. Christian was the daughter of a disabled, impoverished single mother in Hampton. Barely educated, she had to work for a wealthy, ill-tempered White widow named Ida Belote, who would both verbally and physically abuse Virginia on numerous occasions. On March 18, 1912, Belote viciously hit Christian with a heavy metal spittoon. Christian retaliated by hitting Belote over the head with a broomstick and stuffed a towel in her mouth to prevent her from screaming. Belote died, and with a lynch mob threatening to summarily execute her and inadequate legal representation, Christian received a one-day trial that was anything but fair. She was quickly convicted and sentenced to death by electrocution. Her youth and the hasty rush to judgment sparked a nationwide campaign for clemency, which, in the end, was ignored, and she was executed on August 16, 1912. (LOV.)

MARY CHURCH TERRELL'S MISSION TO GOVERNOR MANN. Margaret Johnson's and Rosa Bowser's close friend and activist colleague Mary Church Terrell (right, 1863–1954) was among the most famous Black women in the world at that time. She made the most heroic effort to save Virginia Christian, who was to be electrocuted in Richmond on August 2, 1912. As a founder of the National Association of Colored Women (NACW), she was selected at the NACW's meeting in Hampton, Virginia, to petition Gov. William Hodges Mann (below, 1843–1927) to commute Christian's death sentence. She then journeyed to Richmond to confer with the governor on July 24, 1912, to plead for the young girl's life. Mann, who was the last Confederate veteran to serve as governor, refused commutation but allowed a two-week postponement in the execution date to August 16, so that exculpatory evidence might perhaps be found, and permitted Terrell to visit Christian at the penitentiary. Unfortunately, the time was insufficient, and the execution went forward. (Right, LOC; below, LOV.)

Dr. Alexander L. James Sr. Dr. Alexander L. James Sr. (1921–2010), also referred to as A. Lincoln James Sr., was born into a Texas family with a strong ministerial background; his father, Samuel Horace James Sr., shepherded congregations in Texas, Tennessee, and Maryland, and his brother Allix Bledsoe James would become dean, president, and chancellor at Virginia Union University. Alexander James received his bachelor's degree at Virginia Union in 1945 and a master's degree in divinity at the VUU School of Theology in 1947. From 1943 to 1946, he was FABC's fifth senior pastor. He resigned in 1946 to accept a position at First Baptist Church in Suffolk, Virginia, and from 1958 until his retirement in 2008, he ministered at Greater Bethesda Missionary Baptist Church in Chicago. He was for a time special assistant to Chicago mayor Richard J. Daley and president of the National Baptist Congress of Christian Education of the National Baptist Convention. (VUU.)

DR. Y.B. WILLIAMS SR. Dr. Yarborough Burrell Williams Sr., who became FABC's senior pastor on April 25, 1948, had already had a lengthy, extensive, and distinguished career in the ministry when he arrived. Born in Warrenton, North Carolina, he studied at and achieved degrees from Shaw and Virginia Union Universities. He had previously held pastoral tenures at New Zion Missionary Baptist Church in Greensboro, North Carolina; Cary's Baptist Church in Yorktown, Virginia; First Baptist Church East End in Newport News, Virginia; and Union Baptist Church in Eastville, Virginia. At FABC, he introduced both a nursery center and a day-care center, installed an operational public address system, helped bring Opportunities Industrial Center to Richmond, and engineered the relocation of First African from downtown to its current North Side location. (FABC.)

THE NATIONAL IDEAL BENEFIT SOCIETY. The three major pillars supporting the cohesion of African American communities (especially in urban settings like Richmond) during the "nadir" period from about 1870 to 1960 were the Black churches, the HBCUs and other Black schools, and the fraternal aid societies. Such societies predated this period and the idea behind them was to function as a voluntary group pooling its resources to assist (mainly financially) any of

its members in need of help, often through providing insurance coverage for emergencies. The National IDEAL Benefit Society (NIBS), founded on July 12, 1912, by First African congregant Alexander Watson Holmes (1861–1935), is one of these. It had expanded to some 40,000 members by 1918 and is still in operation. The image depicts attendees at its annual session in 1921. (FABC.)

ALEXANDER W. HOLMES. Alexander Holmes was a deacon and trustee board chair at FABC and the founder and first grand master (1912–1935) of NIBS. Born into slavery, Holmes began work at the age of eight as a tobacco worker and was later employed in the Richmond factory of W.T. Hancock and as a waiter. Largely self-educated, in 1887 he joined Twilight Fountain No. 193 of the Grand Fountain of the United Order of True Reformers, steadily rising through the ranks to become chief of the Richmond division. His wife, Mary E. Venie Holmes (1874–1915), established the NIBS Nursery Department (still operational under the name of Junior Department). The society had established lodges in Virginia; Maryland; Washington, DC; and Pennsylvania by 1935. (FABC.)

THE NEW DEMOGRAPHICS. Change was looming for FABC, engendered by population shifts, and these movements of the population would have far-reaching economic and political implications for the Richmond area as a whole. In Richmond, the downtown areas and Jackson Ward were losing population and population of suburban zones on the fringes of city boundaries with the adjoining counties' was on the increase. The African American population in the city was steadily rising in proportion to the White population and the conservative White power structure began to desperately annex sections of the counties in order to maintain their grip on municipal government. As regards FABC, a larger and larger number of its congregants were migrating out to more attractive North Side neighborhoods like Brookland and Barton Heights. To better serve the congregation, a momentous decision was taking shape. (Dr. Kimberly A. Matthews.)

WINDS OF CHANGE. In 1948, there occurred an event that would not only have repercussions far beyond the First African Church community and Richmond but across Virginia. Oliver White Hill (1907–2007, standing fourth from left) broke through the barriers of Jim Crow, which had effectively shut African Americans out of political office since the 1890s, and was elected to the Richmond City Council in 1949 as its first African American member since Henry J. Moore in 1898. Hill was one among an up-and-coming cadre of Black civil rights lawyers of the NAACP who were waging a slow but steadily advancing legal campaign against segregation and racial discrimination. These included Hill, Thurgood Marshall, Spottswood Robinson III, Martin A. Martin, and FABC's legal counsel Roland J. "Duke" Ealey, among others. Change was indeed fast approaching. (Oliver W. Hill Jr.)

THE MARTINSVILLE SEVEN. Roland D. Ealey (1914–1992), FABC's attorney, has not received the historical recognition he deserves despite his brilliant record as a civil liberties lawyer and his legislative career. He first achieved note for his work on the Martinsville Seven case. On January 8, 1949, a 32-year-old White woman was sexually assaulted in a predominately Black section of Martinsville, Virginia, and seven young Black males were quickly arrested. They were each tried by all White, entirely male juries, quickly found guilty, and all sentenced to death. Ealey participated in the appeals process, together with Oliver Hill, Martin A. Martin, and Samuel W. Tucker. The attorneys offered evidence that the death penalty for rape in Virginia had been exclusively used for Black men; White males always received only a jail sentence. In spite of these cogent arguments and international pressure to moderate the sentences, Gov. John Battle and the Supreme Court refused to act, and all seven were executed February 3–5, 1951. However, attention had been focused on the systems' inequities, and change was near. (LOC.)

R.R. Moton School. As 1950 was drawing to a close, some 40 miles west of First African in rural Prince Edward County, anger simmered. Prince Edward, the White county high school was new, up-to-date, and well-funded, while R.R. Moton, the Black school, was old, overcrowded, unsafe, and grossly underfunded. Rather than build needed classroom space, the board of supervisors disdainfully planted ramshackle tar paper shacks on the school ground. Due to this insult, on April 23, 1951, the students staged a strike led by Barbara Rose Johns. Oliver Hill and Spottswood Robinson III took up the students' case against the county, and under the sobriquet of *Davis v. Prince Edward County*, it was one of the cases bundled into *Brown v. Board of Education* case, wherein, on May 17, 1954, the Supreme Court ruled segregation unconstitutional. Change had arrived. (VDHR.)

Four

IN THE
LATER 20TH CENTURY
1950–2000

By the 1950s, First African Baptist Church, after over 100 years at Broad and College Streets, was badly in need of relocation. Demographics had altered the picture considerably; most of the families had moved beyond downtown and Jackson Ward to the city's North Side. As Pastor Y.B. Williams explained it, "The church needed a community to serve, and there was no longer a community to serve in the location at Fourteenth and Broad Streets." The old church structure was sold for around $65,000 to the Medical College of Virginia (now Virginia Commonwealth University Medical Center), and the congregation purchased the Barton Heights Baptist Church building at 2700 Hanes Avenue for $77,000. It cost a further $15,000 to renovate the interior to suit the new occupants, and on June 3, 1956, the move was actually made. The largely White Barton Heights congregation moved to Westwood Avenue and changed the name of their church to Northminster Baptist Church. Dr. Williams presided for another 18 years—these were years that saw Richmond in the thick of the civil rights struggle. Dr. Williams was among the Richmond pastors who provided leadership for the Campaign for Human Dignity, which was ignited by the arrest of the Richmond 34 and, through pickets, boycotts, information dissemination, political pressure, and lawsuits, succeeded in dismantling most of the city's Jim Crow system by 1963. Dr. Williams died in February 1974 and was followed first by Don J. Hayes (1976–1986) and then on an interim basis by Cessar Scott (1986–1987) before Dr. Dennis E. Thomas took the mantle as senior pastor (1987–2006).

Much would change—sometimes quite rapidly, at other times at a maddeningly slow pace. African Americans now occupied seats in the General Assembly, had attained the governorship from 1990 to 1994, and for the first time in history, formed a majority on Richmond City Council, with civil rights attorney Henry L. Marsh III holding office as mayor. But more daunting challenges laid on the horizon.

NEW CHURCH BUILDING. The move into the new church building at 2700 Hanes Avenue was the culmination of years of discussion, soul-searching, and negotiation. A special relocation committee comprised of the deacons, trustees, and auxiliary unit representatives investigated, deliberated, and issued a report on July 7, 1952, recommending the purchase of a preexisting building rather than the construction of an entirely new one. The congregation voted its approval of this plan on February 22, 1953. Accordingly, the congregation of Barton Heights Baptist Church sold its structure, and First African dedicated its new chapel November 4–30, 1956. (Dr. Kimberly A. Matthews.)

NEW CHURCH INTERIOR. Though the official dedication and consecration did not take place until November 1956, the actual physical relocation occurred five months earlier on June 3, 1956. This time period was needed to renovate, refurbish, and decorate the church to suit the new occupancy, a process that was accomplished at the cost of $15,000. Spearheading the effort were Deacon and Deaconess Fred and Maud Tharps (see page 99), who respectively chaired the arrangement and the moving committees and assured that the furniture and equipment were safely and rapidly transported from Broad and College Streets to Hanes Avenue. (Dr. Kimberly A. Matthews.)

SCLC Conference at FABC, 1963. The Southern Christian Leadership Conference (SCLC) was founded on January 10, 1957, in Atlanta in the wake of the successful ending of the Montgomery bus boycott in order to continue, coordinate, and assist in efforts to implement desegregation and civil rights. From September 23–27, 1963, the SCLC held its Seventh Annual Conference at Virginia Union University, and one of the venues at which SCLC president Dr. Martin Luther King Jr. (1929–1968) spoke was First African Baptist Church, on September 25. This image shows, from left to right, Dr. King, SCLC vice president Joseph E. Lowery (1921–2020) and SCLC executive director Dr. Wyatt Tee Walker (1928–2018) at FABC on that day. This was a most crucial conference for SCLC, coming as it did shortly after the horrific KKK bombing of Sixteenth Street Baptist Church in Birmingham, Alabama, which killed four young girls and after Pres. John F. Kennedy met with Dr. King and other civil rights leaders to discuss details of the proposed civil rights bill, which became law in 1964. (FABC.)

DR. KING AND DR. WALKER IN RICHMOND. As the civil rights movement for equal rights and racial integration continued to meet "massive resistance" in Virginia and sometimes violent resistance in Arkansas and many other southern states, Dr. King visited Richmond on several occasions (1953, 1957, 1959, 1960, and 1963), and Dr. Wyatt Tee Walker, who, from 1960 to 1964, served as SCLC executive director/chief of staff, organized two highly successful Pilgrimages of Prayer against massive resistance on New Year's Day in 1959 and 1960 at the Richmond's Altria Theatre (then known as the Mosque). Depicted are Dr. Walker at the pulpit and a scene from Dr. King's last visit to Richmond, at Virginia Union University in 1963. (Both, VUU.)

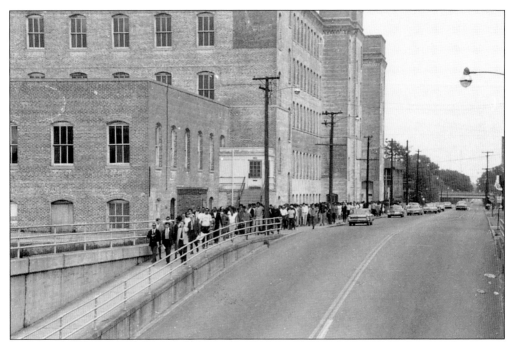

MARCH DOWN LOMBARDY STREET (ABOVE) AND ARREST OF LEROY BRAY AND ELIZABETH JOHNSON (BELOW). On February 20, 1960, and again two days later, hundreds of Virginia Union University students marched from campus then eastward on Broad Street to the downtown shopping district, where they staged a sit-in, occupying as many seats as they could at segregated dining facilities. Since it was a Saturday, the businesses simply closed their facilities. The students would return on Monday. On February 22, 1960, the sit-in was resumed at Thalhimer's Department Store, and 34 students were arrested for trespassing. Leroy M. Bray Jr. and Elizabeth Patricia Johnson, shown here in police custody, were among the Richmond 34, as they would later be known. The students were briefly incarcerated and then released on bond. (Both, University of Virginia Library.)

OLIVER HILL (RIGHT) AND THE CAMPAIGN FOR HUMAN DIGNITY PROTESTS (BELOW). Right after the arrest and release of the Richmond 34, a mass meeting at Fifth Street Baptist Church, led by Oliver Hill, initiated the Campaign for Human Dignity, which organized protests, pickets, and boycotts designed to economically squeeze and shame businesses into integrating their facilities. It proved to be well-organized and, in the end, was devastatingly successful. By February 1961, the major department stores like Thalhimer's, Miller & Rhoads, Woolworth, Murphy's, and Grant's; the Trailways and Greyhound bus terminals; the Peoples' Drug Store chain; and numerous smaller businesses had conceded, and the former capital of the Confederacy was ditching Jim Crow. (Right, Oliver W. Hill Jr.; below, VUU.)

KAPPA GAMMA CHI DEBATING TEAMS

ATTORNEY ROLAND EALEY. Roland "Duke" Ealey (first row, far left), the FABC legal counsel, also served his church as a trustee and adult class teacher and facilitated the move to North Side. In 1983, he was elected to the Virginia House of Delegates and served until his death in 1992. He founded the law firm of Ealey & Page and, in 1961, successfully argued the landmark civil rights case of *Johnson v. Virginia*. (VUU.)

FORD TUCKER JOHNSON JR. V. VIRGINIA. Ford Tucker Johnson Jr. had already gotten into hot water as one of the Richmond 34 arrested in 1960. In 1961, while in traffic court to settle a minor ticket, he was charged with contempt for refusing to sit in a seat reserved for "colored" participants. Roland Ealey served as his lawyer and appealed the charge to the Supreme Court, which ruled courtroom segregation unconstitutional. (VUU.)

STATE LEGISLATOR PIONEERS. L. Douglas Wilder (first row, left), who grew up in Church Hill in Richmond's East End was a communicant at First African and graduated from Virginia Union University in 1951. After seeing service in the Korean War, he qualified as an attorney and, in 1969, was elected as the first African American to serve in the Virginia State Senate since Reconstruction. His colleague, Dr. William Ferguson Reid (first row, center), was, in 1968, the first African American elected to the Virginia House of Delegates after the Reconstruction era. (VUU.)

PASTOR DON J. HAYES (1932–). First African's senior pastor from 1976 to 1986 was Don Juan Hayes, who had matriculated with a bachelor of arts degree from Virginia State University's Norfolk Branch (now Norfolk State University) in 1966 and a bachelor of divinity from Princeton Seminary in 1970. Before going to FABC, Pastor Hayes had served at Kaighn Avenue Baptist Church in Camden, New Jersey (1969–1972), and Ebenezer Baptist Church in Providence, Rhode Island (1972–1976). Under his auspices, FABC and the University of Richmond celebrated the 200th anniversary of the church's foundation. Pastor Hayes later officiated at Morse Street Baptist Church in Denton, Texas, and Springfield Baptist Church in Mechanicsville, Virginia. (FABC.)

INTERIM PASTOR CESSAR L. SCOTT SR. (1945–2019). Cessar Lenia Scott Sr. was elected to take the helm as interim senior pastor at FABC from March 1986 to the end of the year. He was born in Portsmouth, Virginia, but went to Richmond to study at Virginia Union University, where he earned a bachelor of arts in history and government; later, he obtained his master's in divinity from the VUU Samuel Dewitt Proctor School of Theology. From 1978 to 2011, he held the position of executive minister for the Baptist General Convention of Virginia and, in 1982, was the president of the Virginia Council of Churches. In 2010, Scott was a signatory to a historical letter to the governor and Virginia's two US senators to undo the racist handiwork of Walter Plecker (see page 66) and grant recognition to all of Virginia's Native American nations. (VUU.)

Dr. Dennis E. Thomas (1956–2018). Pastor Dennis Earl Thomas was born in Philadelphia and studied for his bachelor of arts degree in sociology and religion at Eastern University and his master's of divinity degree at Palmer Theological Seminary and was awarded an honorary doctorate in divinity in 1990 from the Richmond, Virginia, seminary. He was ordained in 1977 and initially served as assistant pastor at Pinn Memorial Baptist Church in Philadelphia (1977–1981) before moving to a senior pastoral position at Kaighn Avenue Baptist Church in Camden, New Jersey (1981–1986). He was called to FABC as senior pastor from 1986 to 2006. During his tenure, the church successfully undertook a multimillion-dollar renovation project and the dedication of the Poreala P. Goodwin Memorial Organ. The FABC sobriquet, "A Great Place to Grow in Faith," was adopted during his pastorate. He is fondly remembered for his skills as a musician, particularly on the drums. He left FABC to take up the senior pastor's position at First Corinthian Baptist Church in succession to his grandfather and uncle. (The Thomas family.)

Ruth Nelson Tinsley. Ruth Nelson Tinsley and her husband, NAACP leader Dr. Jesse Tinsley, worked closely with First African and other area churches in order to advance civil rights causes. On February 23, 1960, the day after the Richmond 34 arrests, Ruth was standing outside of Thalhimer's Store in protest and was ordered to leave by police. She refused and was immediately arrested. Two officers lifted her up by each arm and carried her to jail. The incident was widely reported in the national media. (Malcolm O. Carpenter Collection, LOC.)

THE CRUSADE FOR VOTERS. In the same year that First African moved to North Side, two prominent physicians, Dr. William S. Thornton and Dr. William Ferguson Reid, and a notable businessman, John Mitchell Brooks, met to form the Richmond Crusade for Voters. It would soon become a powerful vehicle for registering voters and for galvanizing the African American vote into political action. FABC members strongly supported these efforts, and the church became one of the Crusade's meeting venues. In the image, Brooks is third from right on the first row, and in the second row, Dr. Reid is second from left and Dr. Thornton is second from right. (VCU.)

LEAH VIRGINIA LEWIS (1898–1999). Yet another extraordinary lady at FABC, Leah Virginia Lewis, who was related to the Brooks and Holmes families, attended Hartshorn Memorial College and survived a bout with the influenza pandemic. She was a charter member of the Chapter of Alpha Kappa Alpha Sorority. As the last survivor of the original group, she was known for many years as the "Golden Soror." She wrote one of the first FABC history accounts and was significantly effective in transforming Virginia Union into a fully coeducational school, serving as the institution's first dean of women. (VUU.)

DEACONESS MAUDE AND DEACON FRED THARPS. Maude and Fred Tharps were married at FABC by Pastor Johnson on June 13, 1915. Fred was a broom maker by trade and ultimately set aside enough of his earnings to go into business for himself, owning his own broom factory located at Second and Everett Streets in the city. In 1939, they sold the business, purchased a farm in Hanover County, and from 1939 to 1966, opened their farm for receiving and sheltering delinquent African American boys—an estimated 3,000 of these children were helped by the Tharps. The couple is remembered in a memorial stained-glass window at FABC, which was donated by their nephew Dr. Clinton Caldwell Boone Jr., their niece Dr. Rachel Boone Keith, and their families. (Both, FABC.)

Richmond's Changing Face and FABC's Challenges. By the turn of the new century, the old regime had crumbled, and Richmond had drastically changed, Last-ditch efforts to keep the predominantly White, conservative faction with the monopoly of power had been thwarted by the courts, which ordered a halt to annexations and a ward system to replace the at-large voting structure that had favored establishment politicians. In 1977, the first Black-majority city council was elected and sworn in and civil rights lawyer Henry L. Marsh III became the first African American mayor in Richmond's history. Pictured above, the Black council members are Walter T. Kenney (second from left); Willie J. Dell (third from left); Claudette Black McDaniel (fifth from left); Henry W. "Chuck" Richardson (sixth from left), and Henry L. Marsh, III (seventh from left). But political change did not mean that challenges had vanished. FABC, like the rest of the Richmond community, confronted issues of education, pollution, economic disparities, and both spiritual and material concerns that had to be addressed. (Richmond City Clerk's Office.)

Five

IN THE 21ST CENTURY
2000–2021

First African's fourth century dawned with the entire nation shaken by the terrorist attack of September 11, 2001. In 2006, Pastor Thomas resigned from his post at First African to take up the pastorate at First Corinthian Baptist Church in Philadelphia, where his uncle and grandfather had also ministered. He would pass away on December 7, 2018, at the age of 62, and during the interim period of 2007–2008, FABC was pastored by Rev. James Leary. The next minister called to First African was Dr. Rodney D. Waller, who had earned his bachelor's degree in philosophy and religious studies and his master's of divinity and master's of business administration degrees at Virginia Union and completed his doctorate in divinity at Virginia University of Lynchburg. The currents and eddies of ferment and hope have swept around First African and Richmond for nearly an equal amount of time, and much has changed. But one of the most daunting years has been 2020. The 240th anniversary of First African Baptist Church saw the advent of the deadliest pandemic since 1918, when the Great Influenza tested the medical skills of Dr. Bessie Tharps (see pages 63–64). At the same time, the murder of George Floyd sparked a powerful surge of protests and demonstrations that, in Richmond, transformed the face of the city by occasioning the dismantling of nearly all of the Confederate monuments. The hard-fought presidential election and the Capitol Hill coup attempt on January 6, 2021, only contributed to the sense of malaise. Throughout these trying months, Pastor Waller, as an author and highly skilled speaker, conducted services virtually in order to continue the church mission while safeguarding the lives and spiritual well-being of its most precious assets—the people of the congregation of what continues to thrive as the third-oldest African American Church in the United States.

Pastor Rodney D. Waller. Dr. Rodney D. Waller, the present senior pastor of First African was born in Kilmarnock, Virginia. He began his ministerial career in 1998 when he served for a year as associate minister at Sharon Baptist Church in Weems, Virginia, and then, from 1999 to 2008, served the church as senior pastor and CEO before accepting the call to the same position at First African. He is the author of the publications *Leadership Empowerment: Behind the Scenes of Excellence, Leadership Empowerment: A Paradigm in Administration and Leadership in the Urban Church in General and the Rural Church in Particular for the Twenty-First Century,* and *Burning Bright Without Burning Out.* In 2014, he was named by the NAACP Virginia Chapter as Pastor of the Year. During the COVID epidemic, he has been collaborating with health districts, sister churches, and Walgreens in creating COVID-19 vaccine sites in underserved communities that have provided vaccine protection for over 500 individuals. (FABC.)

L. Douglas Wilder as Mayor. The storied career of former congregant L. Douglas Wilder did not end with the governorship. In 2004, he campaigned for the office of Richmond city mayor. A change had been made to the city charter, abandoning the old system of mayors being selected through a majority vote by the city council to a direct, at-large popular vote. On November 2, 2004, Wilder easily overwhelmed the field of candidates with 79 percent of the vote. He would serve from 2004 to 2009. In 2015, he published his autobiography *Son of Virginia: A Life in America's Political Arena.* (VUU.)

MAGGIE LENA WALKER PLAZA, RICHMOND. Richmond monuments almost invariably incite controversy. This monument, designed by Antonio Tobias Mendez and officially erected at Adams and Broad Streets on July 15, 2017, in a ceremony presided over by Mayor Levar Stoney, was actually the subject of heated debate. Some of it centered on whether or not to preserve a 40-year-old live oak tree at the proposed site, while there was some criticism as to the location—some preferred Monument Avenue. On August 22, 2017, the statue was the site of a rally organized by Richmond pastors protesting White supremacy in the wake of the violence in Charlottesville. The monument depicts Walker facing southward and circled by eight small stone blocks inscribed with significant dates in her life. (Brianna Scott.)

MAGGIE LAURA WALKER (RIGHT)
AND THE WALKER HOUSE MUSEUM
(BELOW). Maggie Lena Walker
and her husband, Armstead
Walker Jr., purchased this house
on 110 1/2 East Leigh Street in
1904, and she lived there until
her death on December 15, 1934.
It was during those 30 years that
she accomplished some of her
greatest work, gaining fame as
the "Savings Savior" and working
in tandem with Pastor Johnson
at First African. In 1979, her
granddaughter Dr. Maggie Laura
Walker Lewis (1918–1986) sold the
house to the National Park Service,
and in 1985, it opened to the public
as the Maggie Walker Historical
Site and Museum. (Both, NPS.)

Hilda Yates Warden (1918–2015). Hilda Yates Warden was a true prodigy; she grew up on the North Side of Richmond, graduated from Armstrong High School at the age of 13, and matriculated at Virginia Union University at the age of 17 with a bachelor of science degree in chemistry (1935). In 1934, she was a founder member of the Beta Epsilon Chapter of Delta Sigma Theta Sorority at VUU. In 1951, she achieved a breakthrough against segregation by (after an initial rebuff) being among the first African Americans to be admitted to the graduate social work program at Richmond Professional Institute (now Virginia Commonwealth University) and graduated with a master's degree in rehabilitation counseling (1954). She returned to VUU to work as a counselor from 1965 to 1976 and then took a position with the Richmond Department for the Aging from 1976 to 1983. From 1983 to the time of her retirement in 2001, she served as a legislative assistant for the first African American woman elected to the General Assembly, Yvonne B. Miller. (VCU.)

BLM Protests in Richmond. The murder of George Floyd in Minneapolis on May 25, 2020, sparked a series of nationwide Black Lives Matter protests—and these were particularly acute in Richmond, Virginia. From May 29 to August 16, 2020, there were almost constant protests, some nonviolent and others not so; marches, demonstrations, and rioting broke out in various parts of the city. Protestors demanded the resignation of Mayor Levar Stoney and Police Chief William C. Smith (Smith resigned on June 16; his replacement, Interim Chief Jody Blackwell resigned on June 26) and reform or even defunding of the city police department. Protestors projected an image of George Floyd onto the pedestal of the Robert E. Lee statue (see also page 53). In fact, city confederate monuments were also a focus of the protests. (Both, Clyde Bradley.)

Confederate and Harry Byrd Statues Down. It came on rapidly: The presence of memorials to the Confederacy had long been a simmering issue, and on the ninth day of the protest, June 6, the statue of the Confederate general Williams Carter Wickham was torn down. In short order, nearly all such monuments in Richmond had been dismantled (like that for Jeb Stuart, seen above) or removed by the city of Richmond. This included all of those on Monument Avenue except the Lee statue, the fate of which went into litigation after the governor ordered its removal. On July 6, 2021, the statue of Harry F. Byrd Sr., the political boss who waged "massive resistance" against integration, was taken off its pedestal in Capitol Square by order of Gov. Ralph Northam. It had stood there since 1976. (Above, Clyde Bradley; below, Sandra Sellars and the *Richmond Free Press*.)

DESCENDENT OF PASTOR HOLMES. First African Baptist Church is all about family, too. There are many present congregants who trace their family's membership back to the earlier days. Among them is Deaconess Kim Williams, whose direct ancestor was Dr. James Henry Holmes. Deaconess Williams is shown here with congregant Kelvin Richardson. As Pastor Holmes's great-great-granddaughter, Deaconess Williams thus represents the fifth generation and the 179th year of her family's bond with First African. (FABC.)

Commemoration at the 1876 Church Building and Historical Marker. On October 8, 2014, members of FABC thronged the sidewalk at Broad and College Streets, the site of the 1876 church to celebrate the dedication of First African's state historical marker, which is also part of Richmond's Historic Slave Trail. Dr. Waller and Deaconess Kim Williams performed the actual unveiling. (Both, FABC.)

MRS. HARRIETTE ESTELLE HARRIS PRESLEY.

HATTIE HARRIS PRESLEY AND THE AFRICANS MISSIONS LEGACY. The legacy of African missions begun by Lott Carey is still celebrated at FABC. In the larger sense, the memory of all the FABC missionaries is revered, including Harriette "Hattie" Estelle Harris Presley (1862–1885), who bridged the period between Lott Carey's time and the 20th century. Born in Buckingham County, she was adopted by an aunt and taken to Richmond as a child, where she joined FABC and attended Richmond Institute. On December 1, 1883, she married Rev. J.H. Presley and departed shortly thereafter for Liberia. The mission to Cape Mount, Liberia, ended tragically. Hattie and her infant daughter died of fever in June 1885, and her husband became seriously ill but survived. (New York Public Library.)

THE "MOTHER CHURCH" OF RICHMOND AND FIFTH STREET BAPTIST CHURCH. As the oldest Baptist church in Richmond, First African has been called the "Mother Church" because so many other Baptist churches were formed out of its congregation. (Pages 46 and 47 have already referenced two such offshoot churches: Ebenezer and Sixth Mount Zion.) One of FABC's "daughter" churches figured prominently in Richmond's civil rights struggle. Fifth Street Baptist Church began in 1880 when a group of FABC congregants received letters permitting them to establish a separate congregation in the Jackson Ward/Navy Hill area. Henry Haywood Mitchell became the first pastor. In 1960, Fifth Baptism was the venue for a rousing speech by Oliver Hill that ignited the Campaign for Human Dignity, which would lead to the massive desegregation of Richmond businesses. (Dr. Kimberly A. Matthews.)

THE HISTORY ROOM (ABOVE) AND THE JOASH CHEST (BELOW). At First African, tradition and history are ever present. The History Room at the church preserves the artifacts of the past and records of memories. One artifact is the Joash Chest. The concept of the Joash Chest in churches derives from Biblical passages (2 Kings 12: 9–16 and 2 Chronicles 24: 8) when Joash, king of Judah, ordered that a chest be placed outside the temple gates in Jerusalem so that worshippers passing by could donate to raise money for badly needed repairs. Though replaced or discontinued by many contemporary houses of worship, the Joash Chest tradition was widespread in the 19th century and still continues in some churches (Both, FABC.)

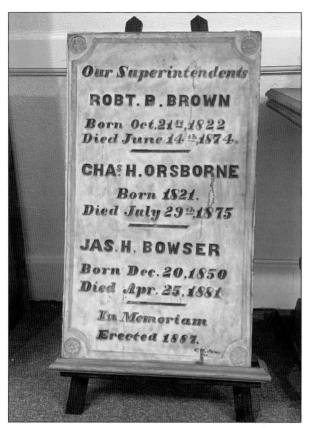

Our Superintendents

ROBT. P. BROWN

Born Oct. 21ˢᵗ, 1822
Died June 14ᵗʰ, 1874.

CHAˢ H. ORSBORNE

Born 1821.
Died July 29ᵗʰ, 1875

JAS. H. BOWSER

Born Dec. 20, 1850
Died Apr. 25, 1881

In Memoriam
Erected 1887.

THE SUPERINTENDENT STONE (LEFT) AND ORIGINAL PULPIT (BELOW). The superintendents served in an equivalent capacity to principals for the FABC Sunday schools. Their prime responsibility would have been monitoring the age levels of the students and recruiting and matching teachers to the appropriate age levels. The stone that commemorates recently transitioned superintendents was likely stored when the 1876 building was being renovated and later transported to Hanes Avenue. The date of the old pastors' pulpit is uncertain; it possibly dates from before 1841. It is intriguing to imagine that it may have been used by Dr. Ryland and Dr. Holmes and perhaps even Lott Cary and, as an artifact, possibly spanned the time of the separation. (Both, FABC.)

Hymnal (Right) and Plate (Below). Among the many treasured artifacts of the past are an old hymnal and commemorative plate. "Before musical instruments were allowed in the church, members of the Deacon Board and the congregation would just 'strike up a tune,' and others would join in, keeping time by clapping their hands and tapping their feet. This leather-bound little hymnal, copyrighted 1892, contains hymns and tunes—words only," according to church historian Deborah Booker. The delicate commemorative plate, depicting the church with its steeple, probably dates from around the same time. (Both, FABC.)

DISMANTLING THE LEE STATUE. On Wednesday, September 8, 2021, a long struggle ended as the Robert E. Lee Statue on Monument Avenue was taken off its pedestal—the last to fall, as it was the first to be erected on this street. In contrast to the scenes one year before, it was done calmly and without confrontation. Despite the dismantling order by the governor (see page 108), lawsuits were filed by certain Monument Avenue residents and descendants of the 1890 donors in order to block the removal, and these were not resolved until the Virginia Supreme Court ruled against them. (Sandra Sellars and the *Richmond Free Press.*)

The A.P. Hill Statue. The last Confederate statue left standing was located within the North Side community served by FABC, at the intersection of Hermitage Road and Laburnum Avenue. The complication lay in the fact that, uniquely, Southern general Ambrose Powell "A.P." Hill, who was killed in Dinwiddie County following the battle of Boisseau Farm on April 2, 1865, was actually buried underneath the statue. His body first rested in Chesterfield County and then was transferred to Richmond's Hollywood Cemetery before ending up on the North Side. The statue was erected in 1892. As of the summer of 2022, the situation remained unresolved. The statue itself is slated to be donated to the Richmond Black History Museum. The remains of the general (who was buried standing up, according to his own previously expressed wishes) may be transported to Fairview Cemetery in Culpeper, Virginia, where he was born on November 9, 1825. (Dr. Kimberly A. Matthews.)

FIRST AFRICAN
BAPTIST CHURCH

VIRTUAL
WORSHIP SERVICE

SERVICE WILL START IN
0:12:35

First African
BAPTIST CHURCH

VIRTUAL SERVICES DURING THE **COVID** PANDEMIC. First African has been at the forefront as regards perseverance in the face of the COVID pandemic and has set an example in safeguarding the health and well-being of its congregation and community. As it became clearer and clearer that the COVID pandemic was about to overwhelm the health resources infrastructure, Pastor Waller acted decisively and suspended in-person services. While virtual services have gone on and FABC has adjusted to adversity and not deviated in its mission, it is looking toward a more hopeful future. The pastor has created a strategic team to facilitate a phased reentrance at the right moment. (FABC.)

THE OLD LEIGH STREET ARMORY. In a development that would rival the story of Virginia Union University and Lumpkin's Jail for sheer irony, the dismantled Confederate statues and pedestals were granted by the City of Richmond to the Richmond Black History Museum, which has been housed since 2016 in the former Leigh Street Armory, established in 1884. What plans there are for the Confederate statuary is unknown at present. (Dr. Kimberly A. Matthews.)

EDUCATION. From the earliest days of FABC, education has been a primary focus. One need only recall the examples of Dr. James H. Holmes and Dr. Robert Ryland at the Lumpkin's Jail campus and their role (see pages 36–38) and FABC's continuing connection with Virginia Union University, and of course, Supt. William White's crucial role in furthering the education of young Maggie Lena Walker (see page 42). But FABC has perpetuated its tradition of learning to this very day, including the awarding of scholarships for further education. Depicted is the July 15, 2018, youth weekend worship service with the recipient of the Y.B. Williams and L.A. Richardson scholarships, Brother Willis Anderson II, with his parents. (FABC.)

COMMUNITY SERVICE. A significant part of FABC's mission is community outreach and helping one another. This has taken many forms over the span of First African Baptist Church's existence. Funds have been raised for numerous worthy causes, and more than a few church committees have been organized and have risen to fill whatever need there was. Depicted is one such endeavor: during March 17–18, 2018, the Ladies of the Homeless Outreach Ministries Team prepared meals for the homeless (above), and the meals were passed out at Abner Clay Park, with the Black History Museum of Richmond in the background. (Both, FABC.)

CHRISTIAN FELLOWSHIP AND A SENSE OF HISTORY. Consistency and continuity have been an FABC hallmark over the years, as the congregation gathers in unity and fellowship. The First African Singers (above) have been in existence for 45 years and are perpetuating an even-longer choir tradition that includes Henry "Box" Brown (see page 22). The historical memory and artifacts of First African are preserved by the current church historian, Deborah Booker, shown seated below with Sandra Brownlee. Historians such as Deborah Brooks and Daniel Perkins Jr. and the church elders are an essential component in the continuing struggle to educate each coming generation as to the truth behind past occurrences and the need to learn from them. (Both, FABC.)

ENGAGING THE YOUNGER GENERATIONS. FABC has always been solicitous of the welfare of children and youth, and Maggie Lena Walker was one such early example among many. Programs and ministries focusing on youth abound and, as depicted above, are as varied in their scope as youth ministry field trips to the Black History Museum as part of Black History Month and galvanizing church youth members to collect and dispatch bottled water to the residents of Flint, Michigan, where a crisis situation existed with the city's water supply contaminated by lead and possibly Legionella bacteria. (Both, FABC.)

CHRISTMAS SERVICE. Amidst all the periods of vicissitude and uncertainty, First African has been a constant, steadying force. The season of Christmas has always elevated the tenor of Christian fellowship, empathy, and a sense of commonality. There is something solid and enduring in the coming together in worship, retelling the story of the child in the manger, the angels, and the wise men and listening to the choir, as evidenced in the depictions of the 2015 Christmas services at FABC. There have been days, months, and years of both uplift and triumph as well as setbacks and challenges in the venerable church's history, but there has never been compromise, equivocation, or backing down when it came to fulfilling its mission. As First African looks towards its 241st Christmas, it can also look back on a history of accomplishment that takes second rank to no other. (Both, FABC.)

BIBLIOGRAPHY

Belsches, Elvatrice Parker. *Richmond, Virginia*. Charleston, SC: Arcadia Publishing, 2002.

Corey, Charles Henry. *A History of the Richmond Theological Seminary*. Richmond, VA: J.W. Randolph Company, 1895.

Davis, Veronica A. *Here I Lay My Burdens Down: A History of the Black Cemeteries of Richmond, Virginia*. Richmond, VA: The Dietz Press, 2003.

Gates, Henry Louis Jr. *The Black Church: This is Our Story, This is Our Song*. New York: Penguin Press, 2021.

Griggs, Walter S., Jr. *Historic Richmond Churches & Synagogues*. Charleston, SC: The History Press, 2017. Photography by Robert Diller.

Hylton, Raymond Pierre. *Virginia Union University*. Charleston, SC: Arcadia Publishing, 2014.

Kollatz, Harry Jr. *Richmond in Ragtime: Socialists, Suffragists, Sex & Murder*. Charleston, SC: The History Press, 2008.

Marlowe, Gertrude Woodruff. *A Right Worthy Grand Mission: Maggie Lena Walker and the Quest for Black Economic Empowerment*. Washington, DC: Howard University Press, 2003.

Matthews, Kimberly A. *The Richmond Crusade for Voters*. Charleston, SC: Arcadia Publishing, 2017.

——— and Raymond Pierre Hylton. *The Richmond 34 and the Civil Rights Movement*. Charleston, SC: Arcadia Publishing, 2020.

Ruggles, Jeffrey. *The Unboxing of Henry Brown*. Richmond, VA: The Library of Virginia, 2003.

DISCOVER THOUSANDS OF LOCAL HISTORY BOOKS FEATURING MILLIONS OF VINTAGE IMAGES

Arcadia Publishing, the leading local history publisher in the United States, is committed to making history accessible and meaningful through publishing books that celebrate and preserve the heritage of America's people and places.

Find more books like this at
www.arcadiapublishing.com

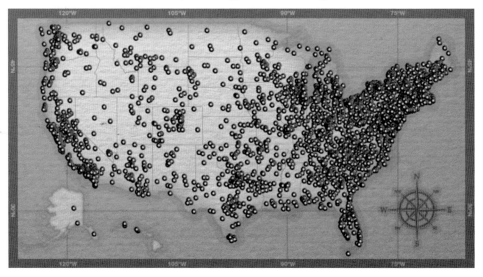

Search for your hometown history, your old stomping grounds, and even your favorite sports team.